EXPLORING
Creativity

EXPLORING
Creativity

*Splatter of Hope:
Become Your Most Empowered Self*

DR. ELLA KARIA

CELEBRATE and ...Continue to Believe!

iUniverse®

EXPLORING CREATIVITY
SPLATTER OF HOPE: BECOME YOUR MOST EMPOWERED SELF

Copyright © 2020 Dr. Ella Karia.

All rights reserved. No part of this book may be used or reproduced by any means, graphic, electronic, or mechanical, including photocopying, recording, taping or by any information storage retrieval system without the written permission of the author except in the case of brief quotations embodied in critical articles and reviews.

iUniverse books may be ordered through booksellers or by contacting:

iUniverse
1663 Liberty Drive
Bloomington, IN 47403
www.iuniverse.com
844-349-9409

Because of the dynamic nature of the Internet, any web addresses or links contained in this book may have changed since publication and may no longer be valid. The views expressed in this work are solely those of the author and do not necessarily reflect the views of the publisher, and the publisher hereby disclaims any responsibility for them.

Any people depicted in stock imagery provided by Getty Images are models, and such images are being used for illustrative purposes only.
Certain stock imagery © Getty Images.

ISBN: 978-1-6632-1355-6 (sc)
ISBN: 978-1-6632-1356-3 (e)

Print information available on the last page.

iUniverse rev. date: 12/10/2020

DEDICATION

A book dedicated to explorers, and dreamers. A special dedication to my pillars of life - my two children Esha and Krishan. Embrace moments to live them fully. Dive into the energy of play as you let your head and heart profoundly intertwine with the beauty of life. Work creatively and productively with others to unveil the ultimate meaning of your engagements. Be profound. Discover what you truly want. Persevere, be brave and be optimistic. Be aware, seek truth and establish your core values. Unravel your most empowered self.

CONTENTS

Preface xi
Introduction xiii

Chapter 1 Self-Identity 1
Chapter 2 Transformation 22
Chapter 3 Expression 48
Chapter 4 Creativity 55
Chapter 5 Curiosity 69
Chapter 6 Inquiry 88
Chapter 7 Connectivity 105
Chapter 8 Diversity 113

Appendix 1 The Emotional Wheel – Build Self-
             Awareness with Emotional Presence 125
Appendix 2 Tips for Parents 127
Appendix 3 Tips for Students 129
Appendix 4 Creating Creative Learning Spaces 133
Appendix 5 On-Line Resources for Learning 135
Appendix 6 Self-Empowerment Model 139

References 141
Acknowledgements 155
About the Author 159

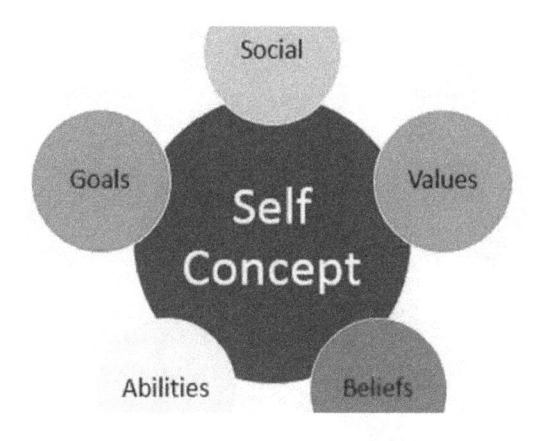

Create a Relationship with Yourself!

Life is not about finding Yourself,
It is about creating Yourself

- *George Bernard Shaw*

Discover new aspects of who you truly are. Begin the journey. Build your momentum and make it happen!

PREFACE

Every individual should feel that they are valuable creators and contributors and experience the joy of the present moment. The sense of wonderment and awe in stillness activates our physiological, emotional, and spiritual sense of being. It connects us deeply with what we see, feel and experience. Finding ways each moment to continue this journey for personal fulfilment and satisfaction is part of life itself. From childhood through to adolescence with the exploration of who we are can lead to personal discoveries and deep integrated connections. It can bring enriched meaning and a clear defined purpose. Expressing the inner world to the outer world becomes your personal reflection. It could start by finding answers to questions one asks or thinks about.

At every level of our personality, we view life. We carry our own perceptions as we come to our own conclusions and interpretations. Essentially, we each have three lenses. At a PHYSICAL ESTIMATE of the world from the body level we observe. Quite distinct from the EMOTIONAL PICTURE of life that flows from our heart and where we use feelings and intuition. Then at a mental level, there is a distinct and analytical INTELLECTUAL CONCEPT of life. Engaging with all levels we experience a natural flow with aspiring and transformative waves. In this inspirational flow there is a sense of knowing.

INTRODUCTION

Searching and defining our personal purpose in life drives us to find a unique gift or special talent that we can give and share with others. What is it that you continue to seek? What is your true nature? At times it is what we identify with that becomes our IDENTITY. Look in the mirror as at these moments your purpose may find you as you have conversations and dialogue with yourself. Reside in this personal energy that propels you to grow and advance. Seeking this true beauty from within, our creative energies allow us to explore new vast spaces. We each view the world with a unique interpretive lens. Whether it be framed perhaps by age, race, gender, ethnicity, socioeconomic class, abilities or personal beliefs it shapes the way we perceive and identify ourselves. We must honour and give value to this point of view. Strive to connect to your identity and find a way to share who you are in your own unique way. Living with a sense of high vibration is a choice one makes. When you show up authentic, you create the space for others to do the same. Walk in your truth. When you blend this unique identity with service to others, we experience joy, exaltation of our own spirit and we operate with full abundance in a holistic vibration with a natural ebb and flow - this is when you have discovered your most empowered self.

CHAPTER 1

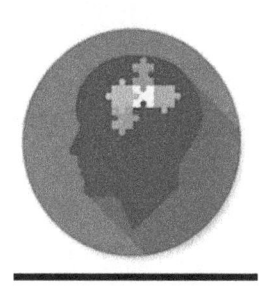

Self-Identity

Change starts with your thoughts. In this era of human history and development, people tend to identify and focus on only a few aspects of themselves, particularly the negative and positive aspects of their mind and their physical body. Interestingly enough, from the ancient technology of humanology, we have at least five aspects that make up our whole, integrated self. So when we only focus on and apply three parts, it can be a little problematic; first, because it limits us. Think of playing the piano with only three fingers, and even if those fingers are really nimble, there is a limit to what they can do, individually and collectively. Additionally, we are probably going to end up over working and creating an imbalance in those three fingers on an instrument designed for five. In this metaphor, you can probably see how an over emphasis on those two aspects of the mind and one physical body leads to imbalances and problems in our mental and physical health, wellbeing and expression. Additionally, how it leads to an over emphasis on what we can see and touch in the material world and what we think and feel, at the expense of other and more expanded ways of knowing and communicating. Now imagine, you are introduced to two other digits: more potential, possibility and creativity! However, those three fingers are used to certain ways of doing things, and their habits can be strong and inflexible. As well, the new digits have been out of use, so it will take awhile to strengthen them and bring awareness to how they work individually and together.

This is a wonderful process, though, especially as applied to our five aspects metaphor, as we can learn so much from this experience of growth through transformation, reflection, practice, and discovery. A sense of humour, compassion, patience, acceptance, and courage drive us. As those metaphorical fingers become stronger and more familiar, then we can take on bigger challenges, be more creative, let go of old limiting patterns, and create healthier more positive habits. In fact, we have a whole new understanding of who we are, more accurate, more holistic, more conscious, more intuitive, more energetic, more capable of accepting and expressing our gifts and talents. Creating a magnetic field to manifest and create.

Identity, individuality, and insight each human being carries and manifests throughout their life can be your own 'Self I-Dentity' as Joe Vitale talks about. Sometimes it seems we are just the subconscious memories replaying in our mind. But there is more to you than that.

If we seek we can experience our true identity, highest consciousness, deepest peace and fulfilment, and our true potential. There is a natural rhythm, an intelligence in our own energy field. However, we must move beyond taking our own field of vision for the limits of the world. According to Joe Vitale in his book, *Zero Limits,* every second millions of bits of information flood in through our senses. I believe at a specific moment we may feel the connection of the physical, emotional and intellectual being merged. This will provide answers that guide you and carry you in a new wave leading to a new empowered direction of being. It may show up in the music you listen to, the people you meet, or the bird that flies and sits in front of you. Look for signs they are there. Move into silence and listen. It is time to discover your personal essence, your inner most true nature, the one from the source, that uniqueness that is yours!

For all the students in elementary school, middle school, high school, and university, you are young and full of exuberance. You are the young adults of the next generation, continue to develop divergent thinking, be inventive and imaginative in your pursuits in life. Build a sense of compassion and care about those around you and find ways to express your compassion in what you choose to do each day. In your gaze, in your stance, in your speech and thoughts. By building awareness and compassion in how you connect holistically, using all your senses, looking at all five aspects of one's self with the world. Create a personal vision and design your future and remember it is an organic state and it will keep evolving. As you connect more fully with people, places and experiences as you become more present. In this presence you connect physically, emotionally, intellectually. You reflect and contemplate. Take the time to meditate and connect with yourself throughout your journey. Listen to your inner voice and it will guide you. Remember it is ok to not be ok. Explore all five senses – sight, sound, touch, feel and smell that integrates and builds a way of mindful and enjoyable living in each moment. Just acknowledge and label what it is that you are feeling.

What are the five aspects of your SELF? There is the Physical, Intellectual, Emotional, Social and Spiritual (PIESS) SELF. In the spiritual SELF you need to access your suprasense." Engage with the 'superasense' – your intuitive power as this is the most powerful one. Gain access to who you truly are by understanding how you can tap into access points and open up to receive greater knowledge to empower yourself. Explore states of consciousness and seek clarity in your vision. This book encourages youth, educators, parents and individuals seeking clarity on their dreams. Visualize the plan to fufill your dreams.

Explore the Self-Empowerment Toolkit

To be present is to know what you need to know in the moment. To be present to something is to allow the moment, the person, the idea, or the situation to change you. For the leaders of tomorrow, be brave, be strong, establish your values. As new leaders your novel approaches, interesting ideas, and innovative practices is what is needed to build capacity, offer new solutions during challenging times. This is the time to interrupt, dismantle and rebuild. This is an era to advocate for equity and justice. Accessibility is more powerful than ever before. For the future it is the young minds that have unique potentials, creative and critical thinking with the knowledge of technology and artificial intelligence they will engage us as they persevere to discover new pathways that have not been discovered in the past. The new remedies call for creative thinkers and solutions to make our lives more efficient and meaningful. We must expand and broaden the spectrum of human experience at a global, national, and individual level as we have seen what is happening in other parts of the world do have an impact on our lives. We are truly one global community connected in so many ways and this is what 2020 has taught us.

To navigate these unprecedented times we need tools to keep you strong, resilient and balanced. Our times call for us to build our community with deep roots to surround and embrace us as this safety net will carry us when we need a shoulder to lean on. Negativity is caused by the accumulation of psychological time and denial of the present. The unease, anxiety, tension, stress and worry are all forms of fear. We need to rethink the way we learn, teach, work and live.

My vision for this book is to provide a guide to empower youth. The *Self-Empowerment Toolkit* has five key tools to help manifest your most empowered self. Firstly, establishing *values* that allows you to surround yourself with a guiding base builds a platform to stand on. Secondly, *mindfulness* brings a presence of mind in every thought, action and behaviour to build consistency and confidence in your way of living. Thirdly, *self-regulation* empowers an individual to become wiser, self-sufficient and independent as they navigate the challenges, the uncertainty that lies ahead. Fourthly, a practice that is empowering is having *meditative moments*. At the start of your day set your intentions and start with clarity in your mind by establishing a calm state of mind. Lastly, examining *emotional presence* and feelings is an important element that drives and motivates what we do. Creating your own joy and happiness by simply embodying the mindset to live in this space more often than not. To keep the mind space open and equanimous, we need some form of contemplative practice. Learn how to empty the mind and fill the heart.

Explore these five tools to connect more deeply and fully in the present moment. The discovery of self is a journey and process and using these tools will get you started. It is time to discover and define your uniqueness. Create a vision board. Seek the interest in learning who you truly are. Plant a seed and watch it grow. Dream, enjoy the love, laughter and liveliness you will encounter along the way. Explore the five points in the Self-Empowerment Toolkit. Use these marvelous tools to reveal, create and grow.

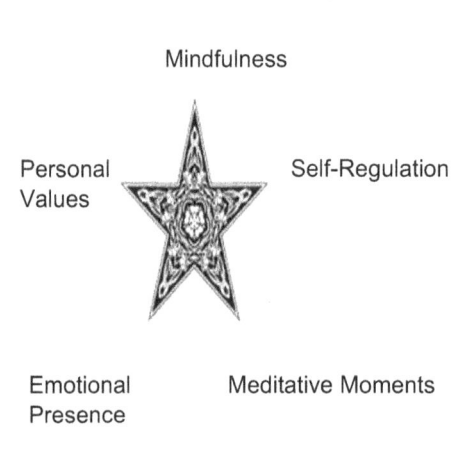

Mindfulness

Personal Values

Self-Regulation

Emotional Presence

Meditative Moments

Self-Empowerment ToolKit

1. Values

2. Mindfulness

3. Self-Regulation

4. Meditative Moments

5. Establish Emotional Presence

Tool #1: Establishing Values

Dig a little deeper. What are your beliefs? What do you value? Human values can flourish in people and communities bringing a sense of connectedness. Deepening the connection with your authentic self is believed to enhance one's relationship with others. As we respect all people and the natural environment, we shift our attitudes, enhance our clarity of mind and cultivate wisdom that lasts and leaves an impression. Children may follow the value system that parents have chosen to follow. It could be guided by spirituality, practices or traditions or it may be guided by the way one lives life. We may follow some beliefs because they are significant to us personally others may not be so important. Try to define your top three values in your life, in your relationships, in your relation to the world around you. Human values are the attributes and qualities at the very heart of humanity, representing the highest expression of the human spirit. Valuing individuals and instilling a stronger sense of inclusivity builds openness and less conformity. Exploring this a little further can help define them better. Educational institutions can assess and consciously identify core values and each teacher and student can also do the same. Seeking for a deeper purpose as you take time to clarify values. You may be enlightened by what matters most. This can help empower who you truly are.

Deepening connections and learning for students means moving from teaching students what to think to teaching them how to think. Teaching children to think critically and reflectively is transforming students' concept of self, others and the world. Stronger bonds and connections provide stronger conviction and commitment. Developing as global citizens, students are compassionate, caring and responsible individuals broaden their understanding of the world and build awareness of how the interconnectedness of what happens elsewhere can also affect you. We can experience this human interconnectedness. With a sense of mindfulness, kindness and self-regulation today's youth are more than ever exploring, questioning and transforming thinking about themselves and the world around them. They have a fascination with understanding the lives of those around the globe and how they can deeply connect to the bigger story of life. What makes one unique and different from others? What are the thoughts, opinions, attributes, cognitive, emotional, social, physical and cultural differences that currently exist and where is it that they want them to exist? Youth of today believe in justice, fairness, inclusiveness, friendship, and positive relationships that bring a sense of belonging. With a strong desire to keep our environment sustainable with minimalistic and simplistic living the way you live and what you do will be defined by you. Being aware and conscious of the direction you want to move clarifies a vision. In stillness, we feel, process, perceive and listen. Where do you want to go? What causes resonate with who you are and what you believe is important? Who do you want to help?

Tool #2: Establishing Mindfulness

Mind is man or woman. As the mind, so is the individual. If the mind is disturbed, the individual is disturbed. If the mind is good, the individual is good. Working with the mind we can reframe the state of our mind. Research (Schonert-Reichl & Lawlor, 2010; Paulsen & Sayeski, 2013) shows increasing the use of mindfulness techniques with students and there are many benefits to practicing mindfulness. Mindfulness and meditation begins naturally for children. Being fully in the present moment, children learn how to manage their emotions, make choices and express themselves. From a young age, self-control and self-regulation skills children develop gradually and throughout their childhood (Diamond & Lee, 2011). During my research, the effects of mindfulness on Kindergarten children, results showed significant positive effects on emotional regulation, state of presence, connection to one's own feelings, ability to let things go, improved communication and behaviour outcomes. There were marked connections and positive effects on executive functioning skills, optimism, social competence and self-concept. With students in higher grades there were improvements with self-management skills, including self-monitoring, self-evaluation and self-reinforcing. Simple moments of 'PAUSE' enhanced self-confidence and developed a sense of mastery over personal emotions, reactions, actions, thoughts and managing the environment. With heightened awareness, there is clarity in the mind. During the move to online learning during the pandemic students especially needed techniques to manage and cope with the new norm. Sometimes life brings us challenges and having the right tools to help you along can make the world of difference.

Mindfulness education in schools has been increasingly supported, based on evidence linking it with an increase in optimism, social competence and self-concept for students (Schonert-Reichl & Lawlor, 2010). There is a great deal of scientific evidence supporting the positive effects on the brain and the body. Implementing a mindfulness program for educators also had many benefits. Research results showed significant ease in managing daily demands, stronger resilience, better organization, and gaining of a varied perspective.

Being mindful can help one to access parts of the mind that deal with focus, decision-making, self-regulation and creativity. Teachers reported planning better lessons, improved listening and communication approaches, being able to more effectively get messages across, improvements in concept development and lessons delivery for differentiated learners. When we learn to pause and be present, we find our calm, our center, and our peace. When children feel small in a world so big. They calm their mind, their body and their breath. They create and use their imagination. From my experience children from Kindergarten to Grade 5 enjoyed mindfulness time. I also arranged yoga, meditation and mindfulness classes during lunch hour for staff at our school and they found it most beneficial. So close your eyes and make room in their mind, then move to your heart - use your heart centre to begin to imagine. Give mindfulness a moment in your life. With a profound sense of relaxation and a harmony and greater sense of awareness, simple experiences can leave a profound and lasting impression. Marvelling in the miracles of life. I found each morning and night, I would focus on positive memories, the freshness of a walk in nature, the joy from the sound of birds, the rays of sunshine brightening our wondrous world. For each individual it may be different things that help you along. I have seen youth escape with music as this deeply connects them to understanding the world.

Tool #3: Establishing Self-Regulation

Over the past decade my research (Fredickson, 2001; Huntsinger, 2013) observations have shown that the development and understanding of self-regulation in the early years lays a foundation for higher metacognitive functions. Students' emotional states in the classroom are a part of their learning. When students associate their learning environment with positive feelings, they are more engaged in learning. As happiness broadens one's scope of attention, a happy, optimistic mood is associated with clear, focused and creative thinking. Overall, developing executive functioning skills build self-confidence. Identity skills along with emotion identification skills promote self-regulation that can be developed with the use of mindfulness training.

A wide range of practices and activities can engage our physical, emotional, and spiritual aspects of our lives as we care for ourselves. Bringing a sense of balance and maintaining our mind, body and spirit. – Thinking, feeling, and behaving contributes to our overall "wellness" and mental health. This acknowledgement of interconnectedness of the mind, body and spirit is linked to the way we express ourselves. Psychologist Robert Plutchik (2003) states there are 8 basic emotions: joy, trust, fear, surprise, sadness, anticipation, anger and disgust. Awareness of how these emotions work and how they relate to one another and how one can turn into another brings clarity to emotions, self-regulation and emotional regulation. Adapting the emotional wheel (see *Appendix 1*) to help students identify what they are feeling and how that is related to their energies.

Enabling students to change their energy levels to respond efficiently and effectively to everyday challenges they face will enhance their capacity to learn and develop the skills necessary to deal with life's challenges. I have seen how intense negative emotions such as anger, frustration, sadness and anxiety can consume energy making a child feel tired and unfocused. However, positive emotions such as interest, curiosity, and happiness generate energy. In the Kindergarten classroom, emotions were discussed to better understand and make sense of how one was feeling. Labelling the feeling and finding ways to heighten emotional awareness and teaching techniques for self-regulation helped children navigate life's challenges with a little more ease. In the grade 5 classroom, exploring the emotional wheel and understanding how if we feel a certain way we may think a particular way explored inner connections, creative writing, using art such as watercolours, drawings, drama and dance shared insight on understanding oneself in a different way and allowed for broadened emotional connections. Junior students also were excited exploring creativity.

The awareness of *overstimulation* and the feeling of becoming overwhelmed is telling us that it is just too much to handle. This can affect our ability to focus, distance us from enjoying supportive relationships, be a barrier to finding our inner peace. It can cause an overall discomfort and even a *hyperarousal* that can release negative emotions. Are we becoming hypersensitive as a result? On the other hand, there is comfort and strength in emotional bonds and they will lead you to building coping mechanism and understanding emotional attunement. Human have bonded and communicated by emotional attunement for thousands of years before we even had verbal language. Although we fool ourselves with words, it is body language, facial expressions, tone of voice that actually most influence our emotional attunement. Try sitting beside someone who is angry and then try sitting beside someone who is in a happy place. It just feels different.

Parents can simply connect more deeply with their children with a soft and still gaze into their eyes. Building this intimacy

EXPLORING CREATIVITY

in relationships with loved ones can ease the feeling of being overwhelmed. Eye contact is the principal source of intimacy throughout our lives. Deepen your connection without talking and just being. Begin with a gradual and natural gaze at your child's pace. Students, you too can build comfort by letting your eyes gaze for longer and longer periods of time to those you feel close to and those you feel you can trust. This will help manage vulnerabilities and shift perceptions. Eye gazing deepens your connections with others without talking. The bottom line is, think connection, not communication. Research shows that people work at their best, with maximum concentration and efficiency, when their relationships are the strongest.

During a book talk with teachers during our lunch hour we often were able to choose a book and read a chapter and then meet to discuss the topics covered during our lunch hour. That time to connect and dialogue over the book's by Dr. Stuart Shanker, *Self-Regulation* and *Calm, Alert, and Learning* and building awareness that we are seeing a generation of children and teens with excessively high levels of stress, and physical health problems. A time where children and teens are living through a pandemic, protests and politics like at a completely different level of adversity, conflict and challenge for the first time in history. During movements in the past we have seen how the arts whether it be painting, poetry, music, dance or drama travelled with us through unprecedented times. How do we deal with maintaining a balance when we start to see cracks on the walls, a weakness set in or emotional influxes that we never have seen exist in us in the past. Exploring creativity and the arts can channel our mind and energy to give us the calm we need. Colouring mandalas, zentangles, doodle art or having a sketch pad can relax our minds. Physical exercise, dance and movement while playing music can be an outlet as well. In the schools we integrate daily physical exercise each day.

Tool #4: Establishing Meditative Moments

Meditation nurtures the mind and opens access to higher dimensions. A daily meditative practice can recharge, focus and bring clarity. Take time each day to quiet your mind. Sit seated and spend time in quiet thought. In my observations in class stillness and silence allowed students to cultivate the ability to sit and build a sense of presence and awareness even for a few minutes each day. This created the space to unplug and reconnect. Connections through meditations bring you closer to your authentic self. Studies (Schonert-Reichl, K.A. et al., 2015; Felver, J.C. et al, 2016; Metz, S. M. et al., 2013) have shown that students who meditate or have a designated quiet time have better academic performance. With a greater self-appreciation and self-confidence increased empathy and mental wellness there was a heightened focus in class. Seeing children and teens explore meditative practices has proven to have many benefits such as improved resilience, presence of mind, optimism, connectedness and clarity. A simple exercise of looking in a mirror at oneself can start a conversation with oneself. The deep gaze in your own eyes reveals a story. Connecting with oneself in the mirror can be a powerful outlet to feelings and thoughts. Reading David Goggin's story reminded me of the key to personal transformation is simply making time to connect with oneself and all of a sudden the impossible seems possible.

Having a daily meditation practice is fundamental to staying calm, connecting to your source and manifesting your life's dream. Meditation becomes an easy tool to get you to a higher vibration. If you realized how powerful your thoughts are, you would never think a negative thought. When life gives you a hundred reasons to break down and cry, show life that you have a thousand reasons to smile, laugh and stay strong. Maintaining a small consistent effort to meditate regularly made a massive change in many lives. After meditation, students became especially conscious of their actions and feelings. When students were asked how they felt after guided meditation, all students found breathing exercises along with meditations made them feel calm and happy. Being happy, comfortable and relaxed the mind could absorb more knowledge. Rain drops may be little in shape and size, but their continuous fall can make a river overflow.

Working with parents, inviting them into the classroom and strengthening connections with families also created an inclusive, comforting, positive and trusting environment. A survey I conducted with parents revealed that when they took a few minutes to be present fully with their children, they experienced greater happiness. Students felt a reduction in stress and a more relaxed state of being. Interactions are more meaningful. During observations in the classroom, deeper connections in a bond between parent and child revealed the quality of the interaction. The gaze when looking at a child can be calming as in a child's presence we feel a pure energy flow and share a silent dialogue. Be fully present in the presence of a child. How one interacts with the self, others, in different situations and with different people sheds insight to the state of the individual. Joy became the dynamic aspect of being together.

As young as children in kindergarten have found meditative

moments ground them and provide a tool to self-calm. In addition, meditative relationships with a significant person in your life can also bring that sense of peace and calm because being around a certain energy has a certain effect on you. For example, both the child and parent enter a space and place of flow in play or in nature where they engage in positive vibrations and manifest enriched moments. In moments like this we feel magic. Creating more magical moments in each day makes life more memorable. Nature provides a source of calm, joy, or solace. The world through children's perspective can reawaken the wonder and beauty of moments you may otherwise rush past. How do you interact with yourself? How to deeply connect with others? How to relate with the world?

By making time to meditate, you acknowledge you are a spiritual being having a human experience. Create a motivation from an internal driver. Motivation that comes from inside us is a far more potent force. Experiment with new processes with meditation and mindfulness. Eat chewing slowly to taste the flavours and feel the texture of the food. Use your eyes to see what is in front of you and then use your peripheral vision and gaze up and down and around to see more. Engage all your senses when you are listening to someone speak to you - do you see them, hear them, feel their presence - lower your eyelids and for another moment connect with their energy. Through meditation, you create vibes and send in and out energies. Mindfulness and meditation is a form of personal inquiry establishing a personal connection, developing your identity, becoming aware of your boundaries and borders. You can learn about who you are, your uniqueness, and your thought patterns.

Understand who you are by understanding your personality. The Ocean model (Goldberg, 1990; McCrae & John, 1992, McCrae &

Costa, 1987) of personality developed by J.M. Digman states there are five personality traits in the Five Factor Model (FFM): 1) Openness (O) – imagination / feelings / actions / ideas; 2) Conscientiousness (C) – competence / self-discipline / thoughtfulness / goal-driven; 3) Extraversion (E) – sociability / assertiveness / emotional expression; 4) Agreeableness (A) – Cooperative / Trustworthy / Good-natured; 5) Neuroticism (N) – tendency towards unstable emotions. Each trait can be measured on a scale and how creative one is can be connected to understanding one's tendencies and approach to life. Someone who is incurious, conventional, uncreative scores low for each trait and may have been passive, reserved, irritable, unemotional by nature whereas high scorers are more self-conscious, emotional, affectionate, imaginative, original, creative, well-organized and active.

In modern society we have seen politics without principles, wealth without work, commerce without morality, science without humanity, pleasure without conscience, and knowledge without character. Humanity in this millennium has seen suffering, oppression, struggle, loneliness and uncertainty on shaken grounds that we once walked in a straight line and clear path. We cannot rely on existing leaders, we question our guides and the ethics and morals of those in power. We are witnessing a revolution of the inner mind. Our trail and walkways have more turns and unpredictable conditions. We walk in a mask. What is it that we will need to survive during these times?

In this shifting world it requires us to change and to take time to think, ponder and incubate – looking back at what was, where we are and what will be. REFLECT, PROTECT, and CONNECT. Will you be a different person as you build your awareness. This is the time for personal transformation. Check-in and start your plan to change the direction of your journey! Are you carrying a feeling of disruption and disappointment? We have conditioned ourselves to hide emotions instead of regulate them. You can feel better than you are today. Just take time to find shared meaning and purpose. *What is the most important thing about you as a person? What is the most important thing about your life in general?* Each time you breathe in try to find yourself back in the space that you defined as the most important to you. Each time you breathe out think about those most important aspects of your life. This will make you feel euphoric. It can reset you. Just refocus your mind and be fully present.

Tool #5: Establishing Emotional Presence

Your essence, your true identity, the root that gives light and life to every aspect of ourselves and expression. It is our heart and soul. It's where we have leadership and take responsibility in our lives and are relaxed, confident, and decisive about the path we walk. Heat cannot be separated from fire as the self cannot be separate from you, Each of us leads from a state of emotion. Our personal composition, our nature, what and who we truly are exists with us and stays with us our entire life. Make your mind peaceful, equanimous and serene. Carry awareness and alertness to recognize love, compassion, curiosity, concern, contentment, confusion and other types of emotions. You do not have to attach to it but be aware of it. Develop qualities that will sustain you as an observer. Create conditions that will nurture you and open you to new dimensions. Always do your best under your circumstances and find ways and courage to communicate with others clearly with what you really want.

Feelings are internal emotions. Acknowledge how you feel at a given moment and think about why you may feel this way. Ponder about this emotion and what got you there. Words can be mistaken for emotions but connections to our feelings and emotions can bring awareness to how to regulate them. There are feelings when one's needs are not met (distraction, hesitation, despair, apprehension) and feelings when needs are met (confident, energetic, engaged, powerful, passionate). Creativity flows more naturally when we are in higher vibrational states of fascination, delight, empowerment, calm and centred. Emotional regulation can shift the way you feel to stay in a place that lets joy and intrigue flourish. Be aware of your feelings and how to change the way you feel by changing the way you think.

Experiences create the foundation, including but not limited to the ability to regulate and be aware of the emotions in these experiences and then we can truly and fully enjoy interactions. We all need to be well. Caring for others has an impact on us. Feeling others joy and pain can transition us to bring peace during a time when we see destruction, division and devastation. Widening your circle can change your lens and perspective. With pure devotion and dedicated service we can transform our identity as the world is not made of atoms but narratives and stories. Own who you are. Create your story.

During the pandemic, my hope in writing this book was letting it become a catalyst for being a storyteller and exploring deep ideas that I kept in my mind. Allowing faith to flow not fear. While we are going through an array of emotions, three key emotions I kept dear to my heart included peace, love and joy. I visually and intuitively connected with my mind, heart and soul by starting each day thinking 'I am peace, I am love, I am joy' and setting a positive state of consciousness that would be carried throughout my day. Creating a daily routine I shifted, reframed and manifested what I wanted to focus on feeling each morning. I wanted to feel the peace in my mind, the love in my heart and the joy in my soul. This helped me to establish positive and powerful empowering thoughts and feelings that let me navigate challenges that came my way. This also surrounded me with positive creative energies. I realized I am the artist of life and I was not going to give the paintbrush to anyone else.

Connecting with oneself, one's heart allows you to live in a way that allows you to speak from it and live by it. This mystical space reveals many answers. Understanding emotions and the role they play is important for creating the inner space and then you can look also at the outer space. There are some tips for youth in *Appendix 4* to foster creativity by creating spaces to allow for connection. In the early years simple changes such as avoiding over-managing, giving access to a variety of materials and designing a creative space can cultivate creativity. Giving choice and freedom gives time to explore to figure things out for oneself and this can build self-confidence. Tips for manifesting creativity are in *Appendix 3* highlighting mindfulness practice and daily meditations. Use five tools to maintain a balance and access all your potential energies. It helps build resilience and encourages you to respond not react to the changes and situations presented each day. When you feel in control of what you choose to think you shift to a growth mind-set. Starting your day with a healthy mind-set empowers you each morning.

By understanding that we have great potentials and gifts we can begin to uncover them. By believing in oneself one can understand how to build confidence and find the path that will take them to where they need to go. Along the way harnessing creative energies, connections and compassion. Move forward with a desire to think more about how we learn, how the brain functions and how childhood years leave an impression. You will be amazed at the incredible insights to who you truly are.

CHAPTER 2

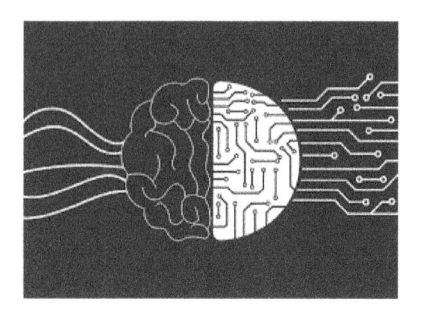

Transformation

> "Your dreams are a preview of your life's coming attractions."
>
> - E. Karia

Creativity is the freest form of self-expression. There is nothing more satisfying and fulfilling for human beings than to be able to express themselves openly and without judgement. The ability to be creative, to create something from personal feelings, thoughts, and experiences reflects and nurtures one's emotional trajectory. Through creative expression students build emotional capacities and communicate their feelings as they learn to deal with them appropriately. The experiences children have during their first years of life can significantly enhance the development of their creativity. The more they see creativity all around them, the more they are able to appreciate the creativity inside them. They have the ability to nurture and grow creative thinking, develop their imagination and explore their inner self. Anyone can make a petri dish for creativity. By making time, collaborating with others and finding a space with the right atmosphere one can initiate new scientific or artistic discoveries; a place to develop imaginative capacities, discuss ideas, explore, experiment and test your thinking or simply gaze in deep thought. By going out and trying something new one can form new neural connections and this is also the time when one is often most creative. Trusting in the natural delights and discoveries of one's senses and bodily experiences can take you far beyond one could even imagine.

Ontario researcher Marci Segal (2004) defines creativity as "an attitude, behaviour, and approach to using one's personal energy for improvement or experiment." It is a separate construct from intelligence. Segal believes creativity is an expression resulting from restlessness for change. He believed playful thinking, intrinsic motivation and flexibility focus our creative energies. The creative journey can lead to a constant call, a strong urge for expression, and an out of the box experience. It can be intense. It can be riveting. Creative people tend to be flooded with ideas. The creative person has a heightened perception, greater sensitivity to external stimuli and an increased intensity of inner experience. It is getting in touch with this personal dimension that can lead one to open pathways, create a sense of calm and deepen knowledge with a profound intensity.

Observations are part of the creative process. When one is alone, ideas may flow best and most abundantly. Creative individuals emphasize the inspirational, dream-like and unconscious nature. Much of the creative planning process is in the mind. As observers, the creative person has the capacity to disengage and detach and focus on the creative activity. At times, they may be watching the world without others even knowing. They have an ability to spy on the universe. How can you unleash your creative ability? What is your creative approach? How can we foster creative thought and transfer those thoughts to fruitful and compelling action. What are you curious about? What sounds interesting to you? It all begins with wonder.

Unlike convergent thinking that produces one right answer, divergent thinking has many answers to the same question. Adaptive creativity is when an individual approaches a problem in the conventional way and produces a conventional solution. Innovative creativity is demonstrated when an individual examines a problem and produces several and revolutionary solutions. Now start your divergent thinking. Divergent thinking is what happens when you find connections between things that initially seemed disconnected. Think of many possibilities. Give time for brainstorming, idea generating, inventive thinking, imaging and visualizing.

In order to build divergent thinking we need to look for what is missing at times. In a story being told what voices are not being heard, what factors are influencing the outcome and are there some hidden biases apparent in what we see, hear and read. Increasing awareness of the power of words and the need to have a frame and filter to build empathy and compassion amongst each other reminds us that once spoken words are hard to take back. Words can hurt, cause shame and fear. We need to recognize that the words we choose to use define who we are. Words can express our thoughts, hold power and inspire. Knowing this and how literature plays such an important part in education has made me realize that the connections to words and our brain and the way we feel is in part what transfers the exchange of knowledge. I explored this with students when they wrote their "I am" poem or wrote lyrics to a song. Each poem is unique and special. Eloquent and direct the writing was a portrayal of oneself.

Moving forward this book will dive deeper into sharing how learning happens. The research and the power of knowing can improve the quality of our educational experience. I will explore brain plasticity, and some of the long-held beliefs, and perspectives of early educational theorists. As an educator, it was important to understand theory with our practice. Learning the background of early educational pioneers lays a framework to be more divergent and develop context in our approaches to creativity. For parents and students the insight on how learning happens can empower you on the journey of life-long learning. Finding your most empowered SELF is about knowing what can challenge you and make you grow at the right moment and in the right way. As we bring together traditional approaches with modern day educational practices we can blend a model that fits for the needs of today's learners.

Understanding Individual Brain Plasticity

Each stage of a child's early years, from birth to school age, has the potential to define his or her future. Building a sense of belonging and deeper emotional connections with others during social interactions involved the expression of intentions, attitudes, desires, fears and likes. Children often learned to co-regulate as they connect with and care about what another child is feeling. There is 'heightened brain plasticity' during three periods of intense growth and reorganization of the brain: one in the early years, another just before puberty, and one around the age of 18. During these periods of heightened "plasticity", many new neural connections are forged and pruned (Huttenlocher, 2002; Ramachandran, 2011). Students being known, understood and cared for by peers, parents and educators supports their development of key relationship building skills needed for life-long social success. These skills begin developing early in life but will need further development throughout the school years (Verschureren, Doumen & Buyse, 2012; Bergin & Bergin, 2009). A student's confidence in their knowledge of themselves sets the stage ability to interact with others and the world around them. Invest time in yourself.

The knowledge of oneself is foundational to many other skills related to healthy selves and self-confidence (Bergin & Bergin, 2009; DeWit, Karioja & Rye, 2010). Early in their education, children form their own perceptions of themselves as individuals, learners, and classmates. They develop a perspective of values and success of themselves and others. It is beneficial to allow students an opportunity to socially share experiences of value to them, to receive positive feedback, thus supporting positive self-perception (Maatta, et al, 2016). Through self-introspection activities, students examine thoughts, feelings, emotions and behaviours building self-awareness. In elementary school science class, when you shine a white light into a prism, it comes out the other side in the form of a rainbow. Indeed, we seek a new perspective on how someone sees us, we're effectively adding another colour to the picture. Instead of looking just at the flat white light, we begin to see ourselves in a richer, more complete and multidimensional way.

The long-held belief is that we fall into a right-brain or left-brain classification, but it truly remains a mystery. What we do know is that our left-brain is responsible for quantitative thinking, analytical details, and is ruled by logic often associated with more 'male' and androgen receptors. It is responsible for sequential thinking, decoding, language, verbal skill development, objective, mathematical, and scientific thoughts. The right-brain is linked to emotional intelligence, imagination, intuition, holistic thinking, and creative thought. Our right-brain functions using vision, sound, 3-D forms, and non-verbal pattern recognition and is more 'female' with more estrogenic receptors. We can access the power of both (See *Figure 1*). Children have peak periods of brain development that provide windows of opportunities. Scientists and psychologists shed light on child development. For peace, calmness and happiness we must be aware that our brain has a subconscious and conscious mind. Our behaviour is primarily controlled by memories of the subconscious mind. We can change patterns in our conscious mind to reframe and ignite more creativity into our lives. If we are aware and 95% listen to our right brain and 5% to our left-brain we 95% of the time we follow our heart and 5% of the time we follow our mind. Engaging in this way we also 95% of the time enjoy the creative process and 5% focus on the goal or outcome. In this state of mind 95% we focus energies inward and 5% focus on energy outward. During the process we develop perception, passion, and obsession on what excites us!

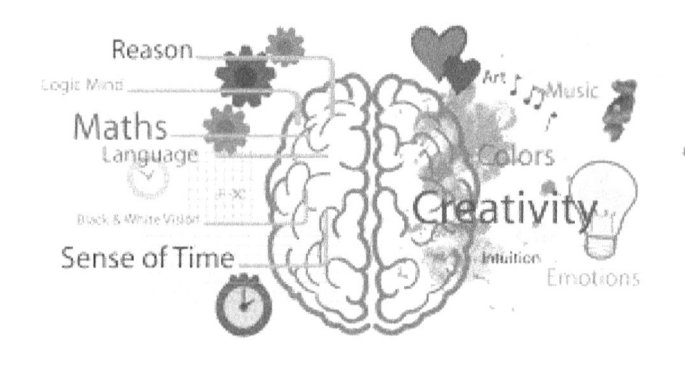

The Power of our Brain

How Learning Happens - Perspectives of Early Educational Theorists

John Dewey

Many theorists and educational philosophers have guided this work. John Dewey (1859-1952) in *Pedagogic Creed* (1897) introduces the idea that children begin to interact with an environment that is continuously shaping who we are. Children are active participants in their own emotional well-being as well as contributing members of the society in which they live. Dewey argued that children are naturally curious. He said children have strong instincts and these instincts are the foundations of learning. It is important to look at the present experience. Dewey (1938), in his book, *Experience and Education*, states:

> Give the pupils something to do, not something to learn; and the doing is of such a nature as to demand thinking; learning naturally results... experience arouses curiosity, strengthens initiative,

and sets up desires and purposes that are sufficiently intense to carry a person over dead places in the future, continuity works in a very different way. Every experience is a moving force. (p. 38)

Dewey's work (1938) has influenced Piaget's work (1950, 1969) and has reinforced the importance of the social aspect of education and the necessity to connect home life with school life, in order to enrich the overall learning experience. Furthermore, these works raised awareness that children's learning does not occur in narrowly defined subject areas. The process of interacting with materials and people results in learning. Education, as Dewey describes, must be focused on enabling individuals to build a love for learning. Dewey's principles of education. Scholars such as John Dewey, one of America's most famous educators and philosophers, believed that one learns by doing and that children's play is a primary vehicle for mental growth.

Jean Piaget

Jean Piaget, Swiss Psychologist, was interested in 'cognitive developmental theory.' Piaget (1927, 1950) believed that children think differently from adults, and he opened the way for educators to explore how children come to learn new knowledge. He unveiled that cognitive behaviours evolved through stages of mental development called 'cognitive schemes,' and he focused more on individual contact with objects than with people. Piaget (1950, 1952) also viewed language and thought as significant cognitive processes. He theorized that mental development took place through three periods from birth to pre-adolescence. Overall, Piaget (1950) set many developmental milestones and developmentally-appropriate practices in early years. Piaget (1962) reinforced that adults can facilitate a child's learning schema by verbal encouragement, physical proximity, and focused attention as well as by opportunities for social interaction and trial and error. Piaget (1962, 1969) also thought it was important to provide activities and an environment to support growth corresponding to the developmental level of the child. Piaget (1972) believed the social support and opportunities for interactions and communication enriched the overall learning experience.

Piaget's Theory of Cognitive Development (1950, 1972) is a cornerstone for understanding how children think and learn. During the preoperational stage (2 to 6 years of age), children develop the ability to think in 'symbolic form' and use language to name symbolic representation or to make meaning of objects. At this stage, children are developing proficiency in the use of language, and are able to think logically and reason in one direction. They also have a sense of adaptation or on-going interaction with the environment, and new experiences add to the child's organization schema. Thus, it is important to allow children to explore objects and learn by interacting with their environment as they make sense of the world by feeling, seeing, and categorizing objects.

Within the Theory of Cognitive Development (Piaget, 1950, 1952) lie four stages, each one containing the processes to adapt assimilation (transform the environment) and accommodation (change thought process and accept something in the environment). Piaget's (1950, 1972) four cognitive development stages are as follows: i) Sensorimotor stage (birth to age two), ii) Pre-operational stage (ages 2-7), iii) Concrete operational stage (ages 7-11), and iv) Formal operational stage (age 11+). Children are very egocentric and view things around them with one point of view—theirs. Only in the 'concrete operational' stage are children capable of taking another person's point of view and reasoning with concrete knowledge as the egocentric stage diminishes. During the 'formal operational' stage, children can think logically, abstractly and theoretically. Understanding these child developmental stages informs us on how they think. Piaget's contributions in understanding children's cognitive development and the different stages outlined major windows of opportunities.

Lev Vygotsky

Lev Vygotsky (1934, 1978) took the omission of the social world of the child from Piaget and the social constructivist theory of child development. Learning and schooling have a highly complex and dynamic relation with social development. Vygotsky's (1934, 1978) main concept, referred to as the Zone of Proximal Development (ZPD), paved a new road in working with the child as a learner and understanding that each child has areas for potential development. Vygotsky's (1978) emphasis on the historical, social, and cultural aspects of development and learning supported a more meaningful involvement of the child, teacher, school, and community. The child is a social being, and Vygotsky's work (1934) looked closer at how we, as humans, naturally engage in our world.

Lev Vygotsky (1896-1934) argued that thrive in an environment that promotes interactions with others. Healthy cognitive and socio-emotional development is fostered through these positive interactions. When children, educators and parents provide cultural tools in the environment for children to accomplish different tasks and become capable of acquiring higher-level thinking (Vygotsky, 1978). Vygotsky argued that meaning should constitute the central aspect of learning. The notion of ZDP enables cooperation and positive interdependence. Rather than rote learning and paper-and-pencil approaches, there is an awareness and appreciation for the use of other forms of learning, including the incorporation of a variety of activities involving music, anxiety-reducing techniques, risk-taking, interpersonal relations, storytelling, role-play, drama, humour, and games in the classroom. These are known to facilitate the deep engagement among students and the transformation that is essential for the achievement of higher potential in teaching and learning.

The work of Piaget (1950, 1969, 1972) and the published works of Vygotsky (1978, 1987, 1998) have demonstrated that learning is a complex process that results in the interaction of children's own thinking and their experiences in the external world. As children get older, they acquire new skills and experiences that facilitate the learning process. Children learn by doing, and play stimulates self-regulation, self-awareness, and self-confidence in children. Psychologist and cognitive learning theorist Jerome Bruner, born in New York and a Professor of Psychology at Harvard, published books such as *The Process of Education* (1960), *Acts of Meaning* (1991), and *The Culture of Education* (1996). Bruner et al. (1976) first outlined the principles of discovery, learning about how people construct knowledge based on prior experiences and then information and knowledge under three modes: enactive skills (manipulating objects, spatial awareness), iconic skills (visual recognition, the ability to compare and contrast), and symbolic skills (abstract reasoning). Bruner (1976) also examined the role of play in problem-solving skill development. Bruner (1967, 1976) initiated curriculum change based on the notion that learning is an active, social process in which students construct new ideas or concepts based on their current knowledge, and his work in childhood learning and perception has made him a key figure in educational reform. According to constructivist theory, we don't just absorb understanding; we build it.

Jerome Bruner

Jerome Bruner (1915-2016) believed learning is an active process in which learners construct new ideas or concepts based on their prior knowledge and experience. He argued children have an innate interest and strong predisposition thus, there is a need to not only teach children what to do but focus on what children are thinking and the rationale behind that thinking. Educators encourage inquiry that leads children to think more about their own thinking and known as metacognition is higher-level thinking that enables analysis of one's own learning. Bruner recognized that children have the ability to invent new things by themselves.

Bruner, Sylva, and Genova contend that "play enables a child to sustain his activity over a long period of time" (1976, p. 244). Play also contributes to problem-solving. Bruner et al. (1976), discovered that those who have had prior opportunities to play "are better equipped to solve problems and that they encounter frustration better than those who did not" (p. 245). In addition, Bruner et al. (1976) described how play influences the ability of the child to speak, listen, read, and write. Thus, it has been established that there is a connection between play and language development.

Howard Earl Gardner

Howard Earl Gardner (2009, 2011), born in Pennsylvania in 1943, and co-founder with Nelson Goodman of 'Project Zero,' focused on studies of artistic thought and creativity and human potential. Gardner's ideas were published in the books *The Shattered*

Mind and *Frames of Mind*. Gardner felt strongly that teachers should take individual differences among children seriously. Gardner (1999) emphasized that the bottom line is a deep interest in understanding how children's minds are different from one another's, and in helping them use their minds well in order to successfully participate in classroom learning.

Gardner's (1999, 2011) Multiple Intelligences (MI) theory raised awareness of the importance of honouring individual learning styles, particularly given students' diverse backgrounds and lived experiences; the student was no longer seen as an empty vessel that needed to be filled. Connecting learning to students' lived experiences had a very meaningful role in the learning process. The need for learners to take more responsibility (Gardner, 1975) led to a changing relationship between the student and the teacher. As children were encouraged to question and think, and teachers were required not to give answers, the teacher's role inevitably became more of a facilitator, and the students' participation and engagement became priorities.

Understanding that children learn in different ways and there is more than one type of intelligence opened the eyes of educators to look at various teaching approaches and differentiated learning practices. Gardner defined intelligence as the "ability to solve problems or create products that are valued within one or more cultural settings" (Gardner, 1999, 33–34). Not only did he define mathematical or linguistic intelligences, but with his new outlook, Gardner also defined types of intelligences that looked at other areas such as music, movement, visual, and personal. He conceived of 'seven intelligences': verbal-linguistic, musical-rhythmic, logical-mathematical, visual-spatial, bodily-kinaesthetic, and personal (interpersonal and intrapersonal). Two decades later, Gardner added two more potentialities: naturalistic and existential intelligences. Implicit in his theory is the overlap of the intelligences (Gardner, 1999). His focus was more on how children learn in different ways.

Rudolf Steiner

Rudolf Steiner (1965, 1994), Austrian philosopher and scientist, knew intuitively that the whole person must explore the educational process. Steiner (1973) believed that a greater sense of individual and personal freedom could enhance perception. By weaving these into the teaching methods and concepts of his 'anthroposophy theory,' Steiner (1996, 1997, 2004) hoped to create a seminal model of education that concentrated on 'inner experience' and the spiritual domain in education. Focusing on humanity and on body, mind, and spirit, he looked closely at each individual as he developed his spiritual philosophy of education. Steiner's (1965, 1994) resulting educational system is designed to foster emotional intelligence, nurturing a lasting sense of self-esteem and creativity to develop problem-solving skills.

Rudolf Steiner's (1965) discussed in his book, *Education of the Child in Light of Anthroposophy*, the importance of spirituality and having a sense of sacredness, and not just physical and social interconnections. There is a greater vision, which not only focuses on teaching techniques and assessment strategies, but also on nurturing individuals in their entirety. Steiner's investigation and development of approaches for Waldorf education began in 1919 and has become the fastest growing independent school movement in the world. It is important to look at "body, mind, and spirit" (Steiner, 1994, p.13). Steiner's (1994, 1996, 2004) advice to teachers was to be creative and flexible, to use humour and surprise in the classroom, and to teach with enthusiasm rather than a rigid schedule. According to Steiner (2004), it is important to build on curiosities by creating wonder and awe in the program and integrating the arts into all subject areas.

Clarity with Connections

To recognize the value of children's identities, it is important to recognize individual differences. Identity begins to develop at birth as children recognize a self-concept based on their gender, race, ethnicity and families. Personal language, self-expression, and individual abilities reveal a child's uniqueness. Identity also represents a child's interests, history, traditions, relationships, ideas and social interactions. At an early age children develop a sense of self. A positive personal and cultural identity is the awareness, understanding and appreciation of all matters that contribute to a healthy sense of self. Self-awareness affects a child's capacity to form an identity and see themselves as uniquely different from other people. In seeking truth we also reveal yourself.

Children come from all backgrounds and walks of life. They bring with them their stories, experiences, history, cultural heritage and family and out-of-school lives. Designing environments to support children's identities create a sense of belonging. Play, curiosity, and inquiry fuel creativity. Children need to feel valued and supported. Allow children to experience the joy of childhood. We need classroom environments where every child can flourish and learn diverse values, and explore their divergent thinking and diverse abilities. The attention to self is an important stepping stone for students to develop empathy and understanding of others and the world around them. As an educator, challenging students and providing feedback and asking questions scaffold learning. As a parent, understanding what makes your child unique allows you to nurture passions, interests, and skill development. We are seeing a generation of children and teens with excessive and high levels of creative potential.

Situating Myself

Like all great gardens, I imagined what my classroom would look and feel like at the beginning of each school year. I set my intentions and refined values and pedagogy to reflect my vision. Then I created the circumstances to make it happen. Planning and facilitating experiences, inviting learners and establishing a connection with students, creating a learning environment that engaged my students to their full potential by developing their whole self. Guiding questions that would make them ponder just that little bit more. Establishing an inquiry stance that would inspire and hone curiosity. Letting students interpret and identify with topics and discussions. Providing opportunities for voice and giving them the opportunity to discover their unique abilities and opinions. The social, emotional, physical and cognitive development of young minds as a focus and purpose to my teaching taught me to support students, parents and families in the community to maximize optimal learning experiences.

With a goal to provide quality and accessible learning opportunities as well as lasting lifelong learning experiences. Deciding on class activities and lessons, planning, creating and letting the inquisitive minds of learners become my guide. As an elementary school teacher, the joy of children's perspectives made me smile. As I worked with Grade 5 students I heard more about what students were wondering about and the curiosities about the world around them. Science discussions always excited students. The opportunity to try an experiment, test a hypothesis or make connections of book knowledge with real life examples became amazingly awesome! I enjoyed working with children of different grades as it broadened my perspectives of how they learned best. The way children could simply and naturally take materials, invent and create. It was making learning riveting and exciting that made my work play.

Exploring educational practices to meet the needs of varying learners and diverse backgrounds in my own classroom, bringing in items the children asked for, brainstorming on how the space should be organized, reading, researching on innovative learning approaches and expanding my understanding of education at a global level broadened my knowledge and understanding. Many students were from many parts of the world. Their life experiences were rich. The culture and language diversities brought unique perspectives. Family ties always held a special place in the lives of children no matter their age. It was an organic process and the creative aspects as a teacher that made my days exciting and interesting. Continuing to evolve, adapt and connect. Rethinking my teaching and learning approaches, reinventing an idea with a twist kept me excited in what I was doing each day. I realized that we must all foster creativity at any age as we have great potential. Developing a life-long learning stance was a foundation in my outlook and instilled this value in students from the beginning and that went a long way. Once students were informed they were responsible for their experience they engaged in their unique way navigating their learning experience.

International Observations

It was during my travels that I started to take interest in international models and systems of education, and I was fortunate enough to have the opportunity to see different types of schools and educational programs in other countries. This led me to join various educational project committees. Since 2006, I have been supporting educational school development through charitable projects, raising money to help educate the poor around the globe. During my visits to India in 2006 and 2013, visiting a school for the blind, a special needs school and an all-girls school and an all-boys school for the poor left an incredible impression. I learned how even schools abroad were honing in on best practices to empower children, and how child-centered learning approaches were evident in these schools because they were making a difference. How social justice issues were very much a part of the daily lives we lived each day. Regardless of investments, advancements and abundance we were yet faced with issues of gender inequality, racism, colonialism, systemic barriers and it made me realize the way we think and operate needed reframing.

In India, many children were taught under trees at times. They were often involved in planting fruits and vegetables to build self-sustaining and self-regulating lifestyles. I was inspired to start my own self-sustaining vegetable garden. Children also engaged in the daily practices of yoga and meditation as a way to practice focus and do exercise. Making me explore this practice in my daily life. At a very young age, children were taught the power of settling within, building strength, and improving flexibility. Meditation and yoga were a part of the school day and it built physical and mental strength in students increasing their capacities to study. My experiences in India broadened my perspectives, encouraged me to look deeper at Gandhi's philosophies (Gandhi, 1929, 1938) on the power of human intellect, and allowed me to compare educational approaches on a more global level. It was a way of knowing and learning at a global level as well as appreciating simple traditions as effective practices. Sometimes we get lost in the new and forget to go back to the old. Thereafter, as a teacher, during my visits to places around the world, I would look for opportunities to read or observe educational systems. Talking to elementary teachers in Costa Rica, Mexico, Hong Kong, Vietnam and Thailand while visiting their classrooms, interacting with local children from different parts of the world broadened my educational philosophy. Connecting and talking to educators in different parts of the world became a very interesting and enlightening undertaking. I also began to appreciate the traditional as well as the modern ways of knowing, both Eastern and Western educational philosophies and approaches. As a contemplative practitioner, I could see how all these experiences informed my way of knowing and equalized my educational equilibrium.

Born in England and having been taught in my kindergarten years in a British school system sparked curiosities to look closer at European educational approaches. During my visits to England, Italy, Germany and Switzerland I learned about schooling in towns that I visited. In particular the Reggio-Emilia model brought great impact and influence in developing my educational philosophy and classroom practices when I came back to my own classroom.

The memories of travel, visiting schools, entering classroom spaces broadened and connected me deeply with children all around the world and building a better understanding of best practices globally. It really got me reflecting and thinking of all the important things I observed and learned and the direction education needed to go. It involved blended learning models.

Over time, I brought a sense of presence in learning and the significance of mindfulness shifted my mind making it a stronger foundation of being. The challenges became learning experiences I cultivated in my mind and decided to conquer. At that time, I was on the path to observe, compare, research, and read more about educational philosophies. I became aware of the differentiated needs of students and the best approaches to better understand their background and culture. Enhancing individual identity became natural once I took the time to observe, connect and listen.

Since 2006 I started teaching in the public school sector as I raised my children but I continued to learn and engage in committees to support and help my community in any way I could. As a teacher and researcher, I have continually shifted my approach by re-evaluating and re-examining my work and paying attention to the words and language in dialogue with professionals, educators, and students. By focusing my deeper understanding of the overall effectiveness of a process and being intentional with words I used I could apply knowledge to my reality. I discovered that it is valuable to have blended experiences in teaching and research altering my language to create exactly what I wanted. Over the years, during the process of questioning and discovering, I began to make meaning of what I observed. Having teaching experience informed my perspectives on how children and youth learn best. I discovered that there was always something good hidden in what I did each day.

Being a Mother

In addition, as a mother of two children, the parent perspective informed my work. During the time of making decisions for educating my own children in the early years, I began to evaluate different educational approaches. I began to examine the way that classrooms were managed, the opportunities the children had, and the best methods of teaching and learning for 3–6-year-olds. I considered my perspective as a female, a mother and how that informed my moral and philosophical orientations. When choosing a school for my children I began to see the underlying values presented would shape my children. It was insightful to have the parent perspective and see first-hand the value and importance of investing in quality early childhood education programs in the formative years.

Awaken and Accept

I learned that as human beings we have the unique capacity and ability to be aware of our internal and external worlds and the interactions between the two. We have the ability to pay attention to our innate human capacity. Become your own observer. As educators and parents we need to teach children and guide them to manifest whatever they wish, to turn every obstacle into an opportunity for growth, to attract and create your reality the way you want it to be.

Being mindful, accepting, empathetic and sensitive can improve the clarity and effectiveness of communication.

Meditative Moments

For me it was a daily practice to find a still and quiet place in the physical, mental and emotional sense to deepen and strengthen connections and relationships. A quiet still place first thing in the morning was a space to reflect and deepen understanding. I allowed intuition to grow by connecting and just listening to my intuitive guide. It allowed me to receive more information. A morning walk became a required part of my day as during that time I was alone, I could listen and bring clarity, I could set my intention for the day and commit to it. Often on my walk I would notice a butterfly and it brought a sense of calm and peace. Butterflies always had a magical presence in my life and just watching them dance through the air so light, graceful and beautiful always lightened me up and made me shine a little brighter just by seeing them.

Life as a Teacher

As an active drama and dance teacher in public schools working with primary and junior students has provided ample opportunities for the exploration of the creative process. I co-lead a dance team to perform at a board level dance showcase. I choreographed cultural dances with students from different grade levels. This provided collaborative and expressive learning experiences for learners. From my drama and dance teaching experiences over the years the greatest successes included students building voice, confidence, self-esteem, overall presentation and drama skills. One student who had not being talking all year spoke her first word in drama class.

As a board member of arts and music board participating in governance, fund raising,, sponsorship, event promotion and donations I have dedicated countless hours to bridging arts opportunities for children and youth. I have also recently worked with the board developing a partnership to support youth performances in symphony, opera and a local orchestra. As I got involved in classroom teaching, curriculum development, committees in the community, and local activities to support the arts both inside and outside the school community I continued to avidly advocate for creative experiences and learning opportunities for students.

Short film and movie production always fascinated me. As an avid film festival volunteer and attendee for many years I found filmmaking exciting and so creative. I did some background work for movies over the summers when I was not teaching allowing me to be on set with the production team engaging with other actors, directors, specialists. This taught me a lot about how to make a film. I feel this generation should dive further into film making as technology has advanced so much and the audiences have broadened to include people from all around the world. This leaves much opportunity for novel ideas to flourish. Films can be powerful, can trigger conversations, challenge prejudices, tell truths and spark new ideas.

Teaching was not only a job for me but also a personal journey that opened doors to fostering connections with so many people, a pathway to making change happen and a base for understanding life and all that it has to offer each and every one of us. The joy of aha moments, the discoveries, the inspirations that kept coming my way in a gentle manner. I deeply embedded myself in finding the optimum approaches for child development through study and practice. The inner desire and search for the ideal educational system continued to resonate with me, and the yearning to learn about different educational philosophies incubated within me for years. There often seemed to be something unique that each had to offer, but finding the one ideal educational philosophy was not easy. Looking at both theory and practice was insightful. Raising my own children and working as an elementary classroom teacher for over a decade allowed me to deepen my understanding of child development.

Being an Educator, Researcher and a Parent

Both my teacher role and parental role informed my research role. During my doctoral journey of learning I researched and explored integrated child development approaches. Then I realized how this research was taking shape before my eyes from the accumulation of years of work.

The relationships and connections I have with others and the personal feelings I have for the people around me help define who I am. Therefore, through my journey as an elementary school teacher, I met diverse educators and worked in five different schools. I observed and heard experiences from educators, administrators, and professionals. I was totally fascinated in listening to people, lectures, webinars, reading books and this fulfilled a need within. Connecting with others really inspired me to begin and continue my passion for writing *Exploring Creativity*. It was the connections with students and seeing them develop that inspired me the most. I always instilled in them the power of a dream – to dream big and wide – as Walt Disney would say I told them, " If you can dream it, you can do it." With grade 5 students I would ask them to close their eyes and imagine if they had all the money and resources in the entire universe – What would life look like?

Quality, Equity and Access

The quality of early years practices made a difference in childhood development but continued to make a difference as children grew and developed. Educational experiences before the age of six set a foundation for life-long learning abilities (Mustard, 2006; Pascal, 2009a, 2009b; Shonkoff & Phillips, 2000); this fact also reinforces the importance of honing on the quality of programs. My research directed me to examine many innovative teaching practices and led me to discover that before the Kindergarten years and after the Kindergarten years child development was taking form and we needed to identify best practices to meet the needs of our diverse students. Activities and spaces to foster and explore creativity can be designed. There are several ideas listed in *Appendix 4* for designing creative spaces. For example, setting up an area with materials that you can easily access invites creativity. Inspirations with music and nature can light an inner spark. Becoming your most empowered self involves taking some time to plan for creative moments and creative spaces. Finding an opportunity to play, explore, draw, design or sketch is a good start for anyone at any age.

I ask questions to students all the time. What brings you joy? Sometimes in class we would put on the music, be free and happy and just dance around. I would have a song list of music they helped build. Music that resonated with them engaged them. When I taught grade 5 students dance and drama they would select the music, the moves, the message and with the freedom to create they would deeply discuss, share and manage differences of opinions to produce choreography that was unique. When we would go outside we would look for ways to gain ultimate freedom. During our nature walk we sat under a tree in a circle and would just talk. I would ask a question – What lights you up? What makes you feel good? We went to a field and they could just hang out, sit on the grass, walk around, chat with friends, run around. Being in nature or engaging in movement worked with different students to generate thinking.

CHAPTER 3

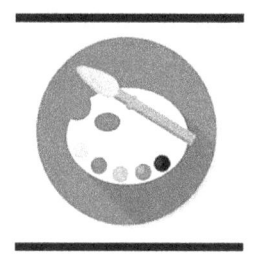

Expression

Imagination stands separate from knowledge.

- E. Karia

Education has taught us many things about following rules and cooperating and listening to the teacher. What it has failed to do is to consider what voices are missing. Teaching individuals to express their opinion and share more about their perspective. What education needs to do is bring forth an equity stance for social justice. Many students have been asked to conform when the system should be open to allow for more points of views. So how can we begin to shift our educational platform to embrace voice, and identity.

The Uniqueness of Childhood

In the younger years we have seen how play opens children's mind for more expression. Play is no laughing matter. Play science is one of the most enlightening areas of interest today. The pure joy and relaxed state of engaging in play is what we need as humans to be happy. Play is deeply embedded in our nature and it is good for us. A giggle, a smile and feeling of joy that transpires as we pursue play activities leaves us with lots to ponder and wonder about. Play also has huge benefits for our brains. Having fun in play is linked to our overall mental health. A recent comprehensive report from UNICEF Canada asked children how their lives are going. The results show only 55 per cent of children in Canada report a high level of life satisfaction, with 27 per cent feeling sad or hopeless for long periods of time. These alarming statistics are part of a key findings from the first baseline report of the *Canadian Index of Child and Youth Wellbeing* released by UNICEF Canada's One Youth initiative.

Our Changing Times

However, facing the reality of challenges, hardship and history may also need a larger platform to be heard. Times have changed since when we were children. Faced with a pandemic in 2020 we all felt the stress and uncertainty ahead. Growing up in today's world has its challenges. Are children in today's society at risk of more harm than we think? Thinking ahead, how should we address the learning needs of our next generation? What makes today's students different from our student years? What will they face?

In play we learn to make micro decisions that could be developing our brain in more ways than we think. Play has a huge benefit for our brains. It is linked to developing executive functioning skills. For examples, kids who are engaging in dramatic play are deciding on who will take which role, and how the roles will progress. There is some negotiation, compromising, communicating, listening that goes into deciding on the roles. The choices, thinking and accepting of roles are also linked to emotional satisfaction, happiness and confidence. Children who have these situations and experiences will gain comfort in navigating and understanding how these scenarios play out. This self-regulation is an essential life skill that we carry throughout a child's life. It plays an important part of child and youth development.

Looking at learning in play at a social level. Sometimes you get the role you want and sometimes it may happen another time but doing the best at what you get teaches making the most with what you have or discussing with others what you feel makes more sense and maybe more beneficial. Those who do not engage in these experiences may feel more frustrated, angry and upset when they do not get their way. Interacting with peers overtime affects perspectives, relationship dynamics, coping skills, and emotional regulation. Play was pervasive, a way of exploration, a way of bonding, and very important development for social and emotional skills. There are online resources in *Appendix 5* that are available to educate, engage and empower children. Emotional maturity is developed when we take initiative and collaborate. Can we handle more controversy and adversary as we grow? Can topics be discussed and debated at all ages?

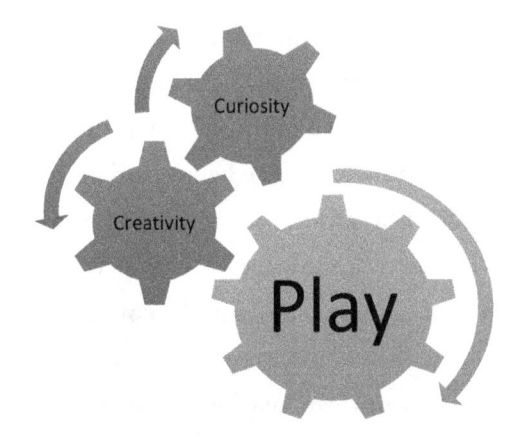

Figure 1: **Creative Development Ignited**

Enthusiasm

Play is the cornerstone to creativity. When there is a deep enthusiasm and enjoyment in an activity the vibrational frequency changes. There is an enormous intensity behind what you are doing. In fact, the United Nations has recognized play as a specific right for all children (UNICEF, 2010). Furthermore, according to the Canadian Council on Learning (CCL), "[p]lay nourishes every aspect of children's development—it forms the foundation of intellectual, social, physical, and emotional skills necessary for success in school and in life. Play paves the way for learning" (2006, p. 2). We each can create a tiny ripple. Again and again we must give space for this process to unfold and naturally happen. Play is natural to us. We must give more time for it.

Play can be the most precious soulful connections in the journey of nurturing learning - leading one to a path of ubiquitous innovation and expression. Beyond the primary years the canvas, the stage, the screen, instrument or voice brings awareness to feelings, a platform to express one's cultural identity using designs, concepts and vibrant colours, a place to play, a podium to share a unique perspective. Riding the wave and power of being happy, and in full abundance. A learning approach that affirms our ties to the natural order and world around us, that acknowledges we are part and parcel of a continual process of accumulation and dissemination to form the landscape of oneself. The self-discovery in play and with a fullness of life in being fully present there may be just what we need to better understand who we are.

Investigation

The process of investigation is an innate part of human behaviour. Infants utilize all their senses to explore and collect information that helps them make meaning of the world. Toddlers often drop an object to investigate what will happen to it. Will the object stay down or come back? When children engage in investigation they collect data, analyse information, find answers and ask questions. The reflective process helps them make sense of connections. The interconnectedness of previous knowledge and new experiences and ideas. John Dewey argues that children must think to learn and that in-depth investigation supports reflection and inquiry (Dewey 1933). Using correlation exploring the relationship one object has to another. Through classification children can classify and learn that some things belong together because of similar properties and characteristics.

Expression

Each student has a lot they can offer. We need to celebrate who they are. Combined with the energy of activity is the pause in between where we reside in stillness, silence and self. As an educator you often observe, listen and make efforts to deeply understand. With many medias of expression - drama, dance, art, writing, drawing, painting, building, constructing, designing the possibilities are endless. It is the moments of meaning that leave the most impressions on us and others; it is the sequence, the content, the meaning behind that brings depth. The personal narrative, the story connects us emotionally, intellectually, socially, visually in a unique way. In doing and being we are connecting but in alertness and awareness we are also absorbing. Being fully present we express ourselves differently in play - one is being fully present with the inner self. In play we are in a unique state of being. Let's ponder - How do you feel in play? What does play mean to you? What value and benefits do you personally feel from engaging in a play activity? How do you engage in creativity?

Imagination

Developmental theory emphasizes the need for children to manipulate their environments in order to learn (Piaget, 1952; Vygotsky, 1967; Dewey, 1990). Children build on their existing knowledge and go further with exploration in using their imagination. With limitless possibilities, no boundaries, no judgements there is a sense of freedom when we imagine. Imagination is the action of forming new concepts or images. This power is inherent in all of us and can be developed to a high level. Children often present a clairvoyance ability as they perceive naturally with an extrasensory perception. They have the ability to see clearly. Someone who is said to have a great imagination can also be identified as highly creative. When we stop and think if someone can imagine the world around us in the absence of stimulation from that world it is truly amazing. Strong mental imagery is associated with creativity. As we use our imagination we strengthen our imagination. Logic will get you from A to B - Imagination will take you everywhere.

Students continue to investigate and research topics of interest in all subject areas at all ages. Whether it is a math problem, science experiment, art technique, historical event or current event students can read, discuss, and participate in inquiry in various ways. In lifelong learning we continue to explore through investigation. Move forward with some core principles to observe, be more aware, and to better understand people and places. Thereafter you can you can investigate who you truly are. Some questions to consider include:

Questions to Ask Yourself To Investigate Who You Are?

- **What do you enjoy reading about?**
- **How have you used your imagination?**
- **How do you best express yourself in the past and present?**
- **What are you most interested in spending your time doing?**
- **What makes you feel a sense of joy?**
- **What do you envision for the future YOU?**

CHAPTER 4

Creativity

Great things are not done by impulse, but by a series of small things brought together.

- Vincent Van Gogh

Whether a young kindergarten child, a teenage child or an adult explores creativity, the value lies in taking the time to do so. Historically, someone picked up a stone and had a vision. They realized it could be made sharp and pointed by chipping away at it. Prehistoric creativity awareness existed when I gazed at the Taj Mahal of India. The profound preservation of history in magnificent carvings and drawings that still admired today. A creative individual could see something that did not exist. They could imagine. As I walked museums in Europe, I thought of famous artists such as Van Gogh, musicians like Mozart, and playwrights like Shakespeare, who went through creative journeys; each one unique and with a personal story. The marvel of the Sagrada Familia in Spain, St Basil's Cathedral in Moscow, or the Notre Dame in Paris - thinking the architectural genius behind these creations amazed me as I gazed in wonder. I realized the importance of the creative process and the elements of design as they hold a sense of worth and place in our lives. As Maslow describes in his hierarchy of needs, it is often this higher level of thinking that opens our minds to creative thought processes. Appreciating wonders around us allows us to find the inner awe within us. We all have innate abilities to discover and uncover.

What does it mean to CREATE?

The word "create" which means to produce or make. Creative people have a passion and pursue it, as they make visible in their architecture, art, music, and literature. Some of the great creators of the past were honoured with the accolade divine. A resurgence and greater interest in creativity has occurred amongst educators in the recent decade. Creative people tend to approach the world in a fresh and original manner that is not shaped by preconceptions. The person may see things in a novel way. The creative individual may be open to experience, adventure, rebelliousness, individualism, playfulness, persistence, and curiosity. Creative people live in a world filled with unanswered questions and blurred boundaries. They may push the limits of social conventions. They like to explore, are persistent and live life with an intermittently joyous tone. Their curiosity may be driven by an energetic quality. However, at times they are perfectionistic and may work day and night. Sensitivities and emotional upheavals could arise. Like a child at play, we must continue to discover what is yet to be understood because we have a long way to go before we know it all.

Through research and practice in Kindergarten, I could see the riches of multidimensional learning experiences. From an early age, a child comes to school each day and is excited to play, sifting sand, pouring water, and pressing and moulding clay. Later, the child enjoys experimenting and exploring, then taking time for sketching, constructing, building and painting. During indoor and outdoor play children often talk, socialize, and interact in a truly natural and informal way. Kindergarten learning opportunities are based on discovery learning and being fully present. Knowing there are no right and wrong answers in this place of wonder and creativity makes it safe and comforting. There are some ideas for developing creative classrooms in *Appendix 4* which can be valuable to educators. The way materials are set-up, the questions asked, and the power of visualization, mood and music.

The child's curiosities lead the direction and focus of the learning. At times, it is their first encounter that sparks conversations, excitement during these 'wonder years'. Kindergarten children have many choices and materials with lots to see, hear, feel, and do. Educators in the classroom are mindful of the natural flow of play, minimizing transitions and letting the process of inquiry learning unfold. Children are happy and engaged. Teachers nurture, guide and help students build and extend their own ideas, freely engage, and deeply explore. Children begin to find their own connections to learning. Tips for parents to foster creativity with children are identified in *Appendix 2*.

Greater opportunities for this type of authentic, quality and varied play are essential for children between the ages of 3 and 6. Children come with an inner openness to ideas and their own thinking. If given opportunities to express their thinking, the individual uniqueness within each child shines. Children naturally invent, create and experiment in their own personal ways. The Kindergarten years lay a strong foundation for success in future schooling. Looking closely at teaching and learning practices in the classroom brings awareness to the best early years experiences and the importance of nurturing imagination at an early age. Fostering one's creativity also defines personal identity, individuality and self-esteem. Innovation emerges from combining disparate ideas.

Canadian Research on the Importance of Laying a Foundation

Over the last two decades, research on early childhood education and brain development has focused on the importance of laying a solid foundation for improved learning in the later years (Mustard, 2006; Pascal, 2009a, 2009b; Shonkoff & Phillips, 2000). As a result, the government of Ontario has made policy changes that have affected Kindergarten programs in public schools in Ontario. The Full-Day Kindergarten (FDK) learning model was introduced after a new law amendment was passed. In September 2010, Bill

242—Full-Day Early Learning Statute—Law Amendment Act (Legislative Assembly of Ontario, 2010)—came into effect changing Kindergarten learning in Ontario public schools from a half-day to a full-day program with a greater focus on inquiry and play.

Policy changes and investment in Ontario Early Years

In 2016, the Ministry of Education (MOE) updated the Ontario Kindergarten curriculum document. Previously it was named FDELKP—*The Full-Day Early Learning-Kindergarten Program (Draft Version-2010)*. The *FDELK* outlined the vision, purpose, and goals of the new FDK curriculum. According to Leona Dombrowsky, then Minister of Education, Full-Day Kindergarten learning was part of an overall plan to help more children have a strong start in school. She asserted that "by giving them more opportunities at a young age we're giving our children a brighter future" (Ontario Ministry of Education, 2010, p. 1). Establishing excellence in early years pedagogy gained focus and priority. Much debate remained on the Designated Early Childhood Educator (DECE) and the Ontario Certified Teacher (OCT) partnership. While both brought specialized skills and knowledge, there are challenges in the working relationship, perhaps because of systemic issues; or just different teaching styles and approaches. FDK partnerships continue to be examined for its effectiveness. Kindergarten teachers and DECEs share tasks and work differently in each classroom. Working conditions, salary, role clarity, liabilities, professional development for DECE continue to be examined in various provinces.

In Ontario, the *Early Learning for Every Child Today* (2006)— also called ELECT—was a framework for the Ontario early years childhood settings written by the Best Start Expert Panel on Early Learning. The researchers from this expert panel compiled brain development studies and compared early years programs from around the world. Mustard (2006) conducted studies showing that early brain development sets the foundation for lifelong learning, and health. Research findings in Mustard's report were based on detailed evidence from the neuroscience, developmental psychology, and educational fields of study. Evidence showed that a child's brain development is connected to early years education and experience. Furthermore, Mustard found that:

> There are critical periods when a young child requires appropriate stimulation for the brain to establish the neural pathways in the brain for optimum development. Many of these critical periods are over or waning by the time a child is six years old. These early critical periods include: binocular vision, emotional control, habitual ways of responding, language and literacy, symbols and relative quantity. (2006, p. 5)

According to Mustard (2006), the brain's architecture is built from the bottom up, and although the sequence of development in a child's brain is similar from one child to the next, the rate of development and the variety of pathways vary. Understanding how children learn best will optimize the early years learning. Shonkoff (2010) showed that genes set the parameters for the basic structures of the developing brain, but a child's interactions and relationships with his or her parents and significant others establish neural circuits and shape the brain. Many brain research studies (Greenspan &

Shanker, 2004; Mustard, 2006; Shonkoff & Philips, 2000) have also revealed that opportunities for children to learn through play assist with the development of multiple pathways in the brain. Over the last decade, child brain development research studies (Rushton & Larkin, 2001; Rutledge, 2000; Washington, 2002) have produced more knowledge about neuro-scientific data than in several centuries. Clearly, the scientific evidence points to the importance of quality early years education programs. It also shows that we need to better understand what is actually happening in the classrooms.

Perspective on the Importance of Play

In addition, the American Association of Paediatrics released a report in 2007 about the importance of play in the early years (American Association of Paediatrics, 2007). The report showed that, starting from birth, play serves to strengthen the synaptic connections in the brain, especially the motor and sensory areas. It stated that there are also areas of rapid growth in the frontal cortex (cognitive thinking, problem-solving, and logic skills), and that children can demonstrate their abilities (Bergen, 2007; Bodrova & Leong, 2007). Thus, this report showed that a wide variety of play experiences is necessary to develop a complex and integrated brain. Research studies (Bergen, 2007; Diamond, Barnett, Thomas & Munro, 2007; Kostelnik & Grady, 2009) also affirmed that play is important in the development of self-regulation, cognition, language, social, emotional, and creativity skills.

In the previous book, *Fostering Creativity* the focus was the investigation and analysis of Ontario's FDK teaching practices. Through conversations with FDK teachers and visits to their

Kindergarten classrooms, this book gathered information that would help one better understand how the Kindergarten practices were taking shape. The Ontario Ministry of Education's FDK curriculum document outlined specific expectations and embedded a play-based philosophy in Kindergarten programs. Teaching practices in the FDK classroom started to take a new direction. Learning through inquiry, learning in real-life contexts, and learning through exploration proved important. Early childhood development takes place in the context of families, communities, and schooling and is shaped by the day-to-day experiences and environments of early life.

The most significant findings in *Fostering Creativity* are that quality teaching and learning practices are based on the following features: (a) learning through play-based, inquiry-based, and experiential-based exploration; (b) making the educational experiences child-centered and authentic; (c) building on children's past experiences, nurturing self-expression, and identity; (d) strengthening relationships and connections; and (e) creating stimulating environments, both indoor and outdoor, for children's learning and development. Teachers' perspectives and specific practices are described, analysed, and discussed. Theory informed practice and practice informed theory, as models were developed and designed during this research journey. *Fostering Creativity* was a great resource for teachers, early years educators, policy-makers, and parents. It highlighted the world of creativity for kindergarten age children. For many children, creativity is said to reach its peak before the age of six, after which it may decline. Art is the language of learning for young children and for our youth. Components of creativity begin with curiosity, inquiry and connection.

Curiosity
Inquiry
Connections

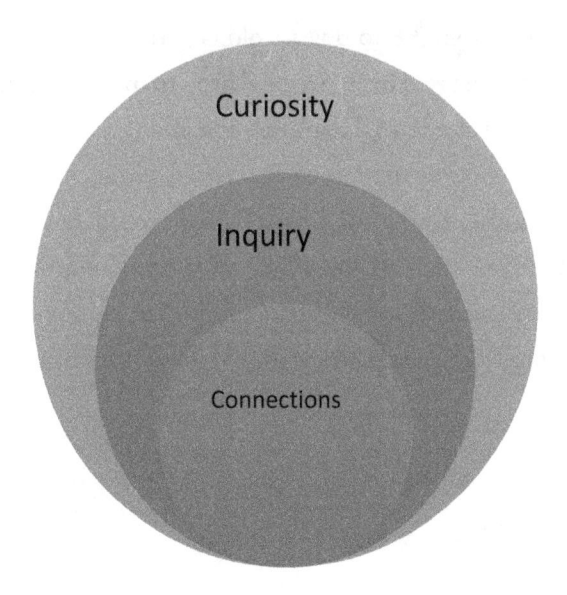

Figure 2: **Components of Creativity**

Around the age of six children, show a relatively high level of skills and begin to overcome challenges, often fostering intellectual growth in creative thought, trying out new ways of thinking and different ways to problem solve. Children at this age are still egocentric, meaning they develop their own meaning without seeing it from another person's point of view. Play is a wonderful way to continue to develop a child's unique perspective, advancing creative expression and meaningful and deeper engagement in what they choose to pursue. Children have a natural tendency to engage in joy, awe, gratitude and compassion, which are the highest vibrational emotions and energies we experience as human beings. Broadening activities, inviting questions, and finding new ways to use old things can stretch perspectives and engage emotionally in the overall experience. Building confidence to share their personal voice, thoughts and ideas can vary depending on personality differences.

The period from 3.8 to 6 years old constitutes truly fanatically formative years, marked by intellectual growth, rapid development of motor skills, increased social maturity, and emotional self-regulation. Kindergarten children are especially excited about the world, alert, aware, high-spirited, and full of novel ideas and questions. Without the preconceived ways of knowing, their authentic individuality shines and illuminates in a radiant natural state of being. There is something truly incredible about these formative years of development.

A Canadian Perspective

In Canada, provinces and territories determine their own delivery and funding models for education. Comparing provinces and territories across Canada, trends emerged on the increased investment and recognition that early educational investments are beneficial programs. They offer a space for children to be children. The OECD (Organisation for Economic Cooperation and Development) evaluated and noted five categories: governance, funding, access, learning environments and accountability weighted against 19 benchmarks to form a common set of criteria necessary for the delivery of quality programming. Comparing twenty countries the OECD in 2006 reported enrolment rates in early childhood education programs and Canada falls below the average leaving room for further improvements in the educational sphere.

Innovation in Education

The research conducted was an avenue to broader perspectives. Developing a ToolKit that summarized the findings by both policy outcomes and outcomes for children across Canada provided a landscape with some insight and studies on early learning innovations. For the purpose of the ToolKit only evaluated practices and programs with the potential to be scalable were included. The construction of knowledge, learning, thinking and reasoning that enable children to learn about themselves, others, and the world they live in were included. Programs and practices designed to enhance connections and the involvement of community partners and agencies in early learning and child care were also included. Examples of innovation can be found on the website https://www.canadianelccinnovations.ca at the provincial/territorial, regional, local and program level. Overall, the project aims to foster quality in the Early Learning and Child Care (ELCC) sector by identifying evaluations of innovative approaches to ELCC in Canada that could be scaled to spread their impact. Sharing ideas and practices, the ToolKit is a resource for educators, policy-makers and researchers.

In this book *Exploring Creativity*, knowing that children are naturally curious makes us realize that this curiosity continues by providing continued opportunities for learning, self-expression, self-regulation, and self-discovery in a variety of ways beyond the early years. Some conceptual innovators such as Pablo Picasso contributed most of their innovative work while they were young. Experiential innovators like Charles Darwin and Robert Frost were more creative when they were older, perhaps even in the middle ages. In theory, then, there are no limitations to creativity. Young and old alike can rejoice when it comes to creativity. The creative spirit, creative thinking invites expectations of delivery and discovery and can be nurtured during the schooling years when there are developmental peaks in childhood and the youth years (See *Figure 3*). The beliefs and value that underlies the action can also reveal and align with the uniqueness about the individual. Why is it important to the individual? What does it mean to them? How will ideas be expressed? For all ages when you leverage access, freedom, space and opportunity creativity affords; the sky's the limit.

Childhood · Youth Years · Adulthood

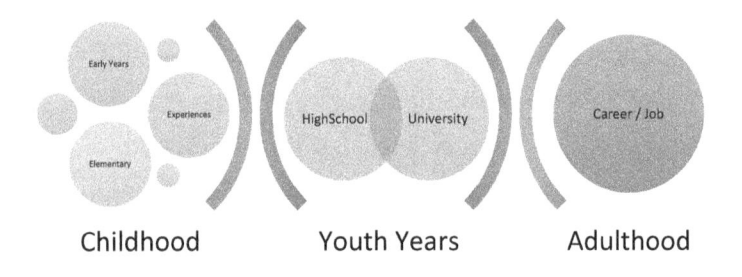

Figure 3: **Creative Thinking Stages – Peaks in Childhood**

The creative process is a natural part of a way of thinking. Development is a cornerstone of the role of the teacher. Can the classroom allow the ease in flow of creative development? There is a uniqueness that arises at an early age that is visible in patterns in drawings, thought, stories created in the classroom. Having the opportunity to see, think, and make mental manipulations of observations is also highly relevant. While at school, students share a glimpse of who they truly are. Understanding one's child, can be enlightening as a parent. Figuring out my own children and what they are all about continues to drive awe and wonder. There are tips for parents in *Appendix 2*. Like a gift presented to you with layers of gift wrapping, you must continue to discover who your children are. What makes them special? What makes them unique? As my children grew and became teens I also wanted to empower them to explore creativity. The creative process begins with inspiration then leading to idea generation, planning, exploring, refining and presenting.

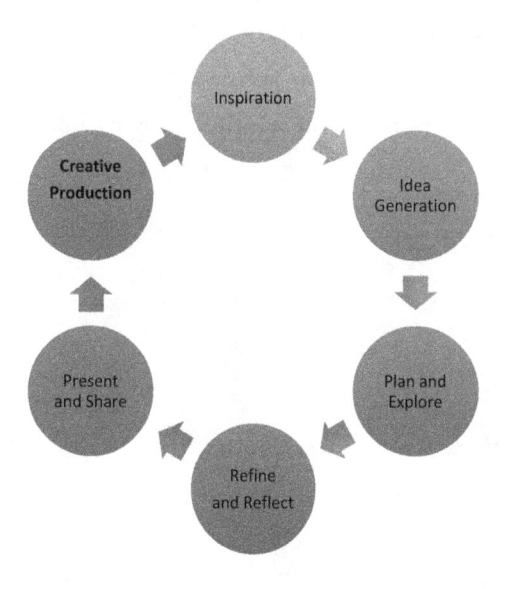

Figure 4: **The Creative Process**

A foundation with consideration of core values, a visualization of a vision and identification of skills, abilities and interests plants seeds and establishes the roots of understanding one's unique self. With life experiences centred around play also support relationship development of oneself to the surrounding world in which one lives. Key components of creativity include curiosity, inquiry, and connections. In this book we will discuss these in more depth. There are questions that can spark personal creativity listed below:

Questions to Ask Yourself To Spark Personal Creativity

- What do you wonder about?
- What interests you?
- How will you explore your interest?
- How will you generate ideas and develop concepts about your interests?
- What experiences and relationships will deepen your connection to your interests?

CHAPTER 5

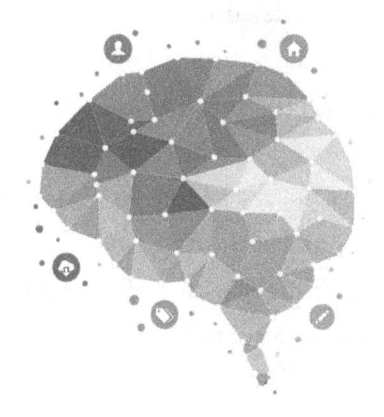

Curiosity

Curiosity has its own purpose for existing.

- E. Karia

Curiosity is what motivates us to learn more. Susan Engel (2015) writes about curiosity and states there is "overwhelming empirical support for the idea that when people are curious about something they learn more and they learn better." (7). Research suggests that the joyful and inquisitive experience of children who pursue inquiry supports further exploration, inspiration, and questioning. Susan Engel (2015), states there are two forms of curiosity: exploratory and directed. We can have the experience of being consumed in a particular interest and wanting to read more and more. Engel summarizes this finding, "learning feels good when the material satisfies curiosity, and such learning tends to last."

Free play thus supports curiosity. Now in elementary schools, spaces are integrating makerspaces, allowing children in Grades 1-5 also have an inventive play area for developing creative thinking skills. In the computer lab educators convert spaces to more collaborative, creative spaces adding in a variety of loose parts, thinking activities, problem-solving challenges enhancing using technology and integrating it with a creative purpose. *Appendix 4* suggests ways to foster creative thinking.

Curiosity Nurtures a Deep Connection

Curiosity nurtures a deep sense of connection beyond the early years. Nature and nurture, along with genes and environment, not only impact development of a child but also play off one another. Educators want to gain a better sense of the learner, their needs and preferences. Rethinking classroom seating, table choices, wall space, positioning and placement of materials, accessibility, flexibility has become more important in classroom design. Access to an indoor and outdoor learning space, greenery, natural lighting, use of colour, organization of materials all are being redesigned. Using a bouncy ball or wobbly stool increases movement and attention for some students. A stand up desk and large group tables may make a difference for students. Encouraging groupings with white boards, large tables and round table groupings increases collaborative conversations, idea development, use of chrome books, ipads and moveable devices provide access for research at all times and not just using a computer lab at certain time slots in the week. The online community, storyboard concept and project design tools provide interactive inspirations for the new generation, who shape critical thinking skills. Students can easily start with an idea, turn it into a project, rethink it, create and share it, get feedback, collaborate, and express it.

Although our brain grows to 90 per cent of its adult weight by the age of five, brain development is lifelong. Brain circuits between the prefrontal cortex and other areas of the brain enable children and teens to tightly connect well-being, thinking, and language skills (McCain, 2020). Creative thinking skills enable the young mind to extend an idea and suggest hypotheses, evaluating information and developing criteria to judge their own ideas and the ideas of others. They also develop the capacity for counterfactual thinking - their ability to think about "what if" and contemplate alternatives, enabling a suite of mental abilities and learning dispositions such as problem-solving, imagination, perspective-taking, and creativity.

Early Study of Creativity

The first efforts to define and study creativity were by Lewis Terman at Stanford University. He began with the assumption that "genius" and "high intelligence" were the same thing. He himself was bright and had an intense desire to learn and understand how the human mind works. Terman's study of intellectual children shed light on the relationship between intelligence and creativity, and his conclusions showed that there is a distinction between intelligence and creativity. Although sometimes creativity can be connected to intelligence it is not always correlated. Therefore, terms such as "gifted", "talented", or "creative" may be different from "genius." A resurgence of interest in creativity has occurred. One essential component of creativity is originality. It often creates a sense of freshness. An individual may travel a creative process working from person, process to product. The process occurs in the individual human brain. That process is neither easy nor obvious. There may be "ordinary creativity" and also "extraordinary creativity".

Divergent vs Convergent Thinking

Psychologists who have designed a creativity test may have a key component that identifies "divergent thinking", which shows one is able to produce a large number of interesting and appropriate responses to probes such as a question or task. It is distinguished from "convergent thinking", which stresses finding a single right answer. Furthermore, scientists have determined that the decrease in play results in increased mental and physical health challenges (Hewes, 2014, Yogman, Garner, Hutchinson et al., 2018, Garvis & Pendergast, 2017). A more expansive understanding of the physical, mental, social, emotional cognitive, and spiritual aspects of human development are critical holistic elements for the integrity, strength and vitality of a capable and competent person. As a child grows and develops into a capable person, it is the shaping of values, beliefs, and ways of knowing that have provided a foundation for open spaces for dialogue. Define your individual vision, values and virtues. Love, creativity, and gentleness within us are closely linked to these.

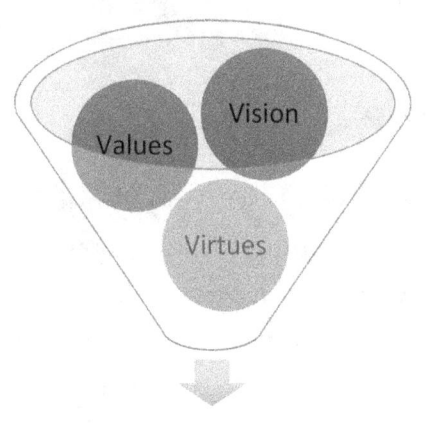

Personal Container

Figure 5: **Who Am I?**

During the creative process, creative people slip into a state of intense concentration and focus. They flow into a state that takes them somewhere apart from what is happening around them. They mentally separate from their own surroundings. A clean slate. Ideas begin to float freely, and they go into deep thought. Lost in their thoughts they move and navigate as they unravel things in a different way. Emotionally, there is a sense of excitement, a sense of joy and a curiosity of wonder. The world, which seemed so grand, so complicated, simplifies into a new form. They travel through an experience, begin to close their eyes, and visualize. At first, in darkness, they think. They cannot ever completely leave that thought because something continues to pull in a specific direction. Eventually a light shines on what exactly is to be. In a dream, staring out a window they cannot leave the thought because it is not yet in its finished form. The dot to dot pattern creates an image. They see things they may not have seen or heard before. Perception takes shape, a new dimension, a new way, seems clear as crystal.

Listen to Your Inner Voice

The inner voice is heard with clarity. Remaining there for hours on end, they gradually float concepts or form. Refining, working, moulding, and massaging an idea by building collective resources, tuning our idea and carving out something unique. Removing, changing, and eliminating parts may be part of this process. As pointed and sharp as a pencil tip, the sharpening process can take days, months, or even years. Slow and steady, with patience and persistence, things inch forward. In the final stages there is a rapid pace, a peak, and a burst. A heightened sense of unwavering understanding to what exactly has to be done. They interpret the idea to its ideal form. Something innovative appears. A clarity of vision. This may turn into an object, idea, concept, literary form, or product. The process of creation may occur in 'that place' and this may be a place of simply expressing thoughts and internal ideas and processes. The process can become consuming. The supernatural inexplicable force we call inspiration often flows from the depth of the soul when the individual is stirred. Mozart describes the delight of inventing and producing as a "pleasing lively dream" it may even occur during sleep. Tapping into the unconscious may be where associative links run wild but eventually create new connections - the imagination is an extraordinary place.

Discover Your Personal Blueprint

Each person has a unique and personal blueprint. From childhood, creative connections develop. The human brain maturation begins in the fetus at a primitive level at the time of birth and takes a long process to develop. It develops through early childhood, adolescence, and early adulthood. The brain continues to wire itself, with each neutron producing more and more synapses to connect nearby and distant brain regions. It is the wiring of the brain that permits an infant to learn to crawl, walk, and talk. During childhood, the connections can actually overgrow, and as a gardener sows many seeds and selects, weeding away the rest, so does the brain create more connections, spines and synapses than it actually needs. It is during late adolescence and young adulthood, a process known as 'pruning' occurs and overgrowth is trimmed back so the brain can work effectively, efficiently, and maturely. That explains why my teenagers are often supercharged. The experiences we accumulate also shape our minds. We become what we have seen, heard, smelled, touched, done, read, and remembered. Our senses, our emotions, our whole being is involved in many levels and in many ways throughout our life journey.

Our brain has an amazing capacity to learn, change and has an extraordinary ability to retain and store specific memories, innovate, and create. Observing my teenage children and their way of thinking has deepened my understanding of the adolescent years of creative expression and creative development. Following the creative process one may collaborate, communicate, reflect, further explore or present ideas to develop meaning.

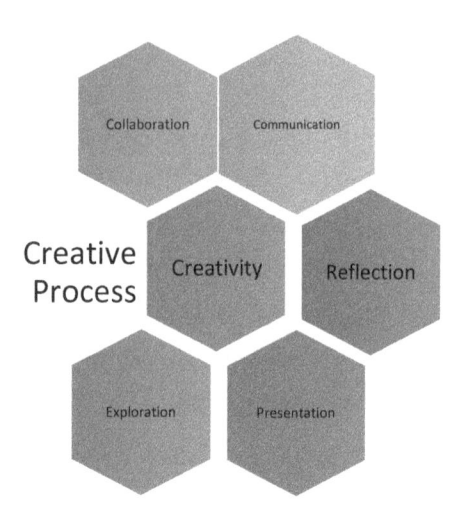

Figure 6: **Elements Driven from of Creative Process**

Everyone has a uniqueness that differentiates him or her from the rest of the world. Crafting a brand identity for each student based on their natural skills, nurtured values, and niche is important. A clear and compelling personal quality stands out and makes one cognisant of learning preferences, meaningful learning, and value added life experiences. Inevitably, autonomy is valued and differentiated learning styles establish fundamental constitutions and approaches. Finding one's true nature brings him or her closer to understanding who they truly are – gaining a deeper understanding of oneself.

Critical Periods of Brain Plasticity

Brain plasticity is the concept of 'critical periods and according to science, there is a relatively limited window of opportunity during which the brain can learn, change and develop. If the opportunity is seized during this critical period, the window may close forever.

The concept is critical for enhancing creativity and for education. The fact that the brain has critical periods in its development was first demonstrated in a group of experiments done by Torsten Wiesel and David Hubel, for which they were awarded a Nobel Prize in 1981. One eye covered of cats and dogs during critical periods of development resulted in abnormalities and never were the animals able to recover normal eyesight. It created abnormalities in the brain that produced abnormalities in visual function. Therefore, looking at human life, we can find many examples of lost or diminished capacities that may have occurred. With inadequate environmental exposure and failure to learn something during a critical period may result in challenges or inadequacies. This is most obvious with the ability to read, write and speak foreign languages.

Studies of neuroplasticity have shown that prime time for language acquisition is between ages one to twelve. The ear can hear subtle differences in sound and can articulate them with their lips and mouth. Foreign language is best introduced in elementary school. Having taught in a French immersion school, it was evident how quickly children could absorb and communicate in another language at such a young age.

A child who reads about a character then can learn to visualize and imagine this character. It is about taking that next step to extend the experience. If watching a movie, the mental visions are already generated and the child is passive rather than active in the brain. Learning during childhood or early adolescence is a time to develop a personal mind-set. While learning should continue for life it may just be a much slower process to learn and find time to do so as an adult but the reality is technology is rapidly changing and so will our lives. We need more than ever to have a life-long learning approach to our daily lives. Similarly, athletes are taking advantage of developmental opportunities at a younger age to capitalize on skill development. Therefore, creating the right environment to learn during the right time is one of the secrets to building better brain capacity.

How Does One Optimze Brain Development?

Knowing that at the right time, the right things need to happen for physical, emotional, spiritual, cognitive, and social development. The lack of childhood experiences, the lack of opportunities, the lack of social interactions, the environmental factors that shaped who you are today. Ideally windows of development provide platforms for optimization of learning, understanding and absorbing in depth and with the greatest benefit, however, it is never too late to try new things, learn a new language, or take an online or in-class course.

Life-long and continued interest in learning is a skill 21st century learners will cultivate and need for the workforce. In an ever-changing world we must become better learners to adapt, be flexible and synthesize our learning to move forward in the times ahead. The pandemic has taught us all to adapt. Our brains are capable of learning new ways.

Nature vs Nurture

Exploring nature and nurture, we may look at environmental factors that influence the emergence of creative ideas. The experiences that children have in life can be carried in the subconscious mind and influence the later years. The memories of places they have been, things they have seen, experiences they have had, and all influence thinking and background knowledge. Furthermore, something connected to hereditary factors or early childhood environmental experiences that predisposes one to become creative or inventive. Talent and natural inclinations or abilities arise in many individuals, and understanding and nurturing talents at an early age can plant seeds for future growth and development of creativity.

Lastly, I believe a cultural environment nurtures creativity. Values of freedom, novelty, and experimenting provide opportunities for intellectual freedoms. New associations flourish and help foster the creative brain. Creative people are also likely to be more productive around other creative people. An emotional support of a good mentor can feed creativity. Intellectual and creative ideas may bubble and ferment when people discuss, argue, and inspire others. A creative person may have idealized abilities in admiration. An ambition, a desire, a defined purpose is an inclination to push further in the direction one wants to proceed. Both nature and nature may contribute or affect this developmental process.

At a young age, through observations of early childhood educational encounters many insights were gained. The ability of a child to observe the world around them and produce original images without ever being taught to do so; as if it was in their nature demonstrates uncluttered thoughts. There is an emotional attachment of joy, contentment, and pride associated with a higher emotional state of mind and wellbeing when a child is engaged at this level. The original drawings and stories are able to tell a personal narrative without relying on background knowledge or experience.

As a teacher, it has been ever fascinating to observe brain development and growth in a child over the school year. Present in their daily lives, seeing the train of thought, the details in the drawings always provided a window into their inner world. A glimpse at the current state and seeing over the year how the individual flourished and grew is like watching brain development in action. The life of a teacher can be that of a psychologist, social worker, a facilitator, a mentor or a life coach.

A Teacher Perspective

Having taught several different grades, from Kindergarten to grade 5, it was often in the role as a teacher that the most discoveries naturally occurred. Things happened without many interventions. Setting up provocations or invitations allowed for open-ended learning experiences that also created space for individualized thinking. No two days were ever alike in the Kindergarten classroom. Each day a new discovery, new creations, unique perspectives from a child opened my eyes. Thus, as an educator, even in a grade five classroom whether it was through science experiments, debating or dialogue it was important to find ways to nurture innovation and creativity in the classroom. We add greater value to the importance of creative learning in the life of a child as it nurtures individual identity. There was a natural way of learning through play. Solving architectural and engineering problems at the block centre would drive original thinking.

Nature is not something separate from us. So when we say that we have lost our connection to nature, we've lost our connection to ourselves. children designed. Having the use of loose materials gave freedom to create, recreate, and reuse materials in ways each and every day. It is proven over and over again that children are capable, competent, and creative thinkers. When students choose the materials they want to use and decide what they want to make there is a power in this outlet of freedom of expression rather them being told what to use and how to do something.

If a creative nature arises in a child nurturing it through a variety of environmental factors will further enhance it. I continued to introduce new materials, set up new provocations, added new invitations, loose parts, changed the classroom layout and integrated various media to areas in the classroom often based on the student's interests. It was like having a room full of scientists, engineers, designers, artists, performers, musicians, and managers under one roof. A scene of creators, innovators carrying original thought, discovering various inventions and bringing them to life as they went through investigations and explorations. Bringing in what they needed to make learning happen.

During this learning, you see the heightened levels of enthusiasm and joy. As children engaged in play, they explored cutting, designing, synthesizing, and building. With a specific intention and purpose, children demonstrate their competencies and creativity in their own way. Giving them time to go back to what they started allowed them to continue to build on an idea. Bringing thoughts into action provides an avenue to discovering oneself and what makes one unique.

In the past, the focus of my work was primarily focused on the early years of education, but as I taught children in different grades and observed at various stages, I noticed that there was a need for on-going creative advancement. This was evident when junior students explored the "I Am" activity. We started with *"I am special, I am important, I am unique"* and then students added there own stanza and created an individualized poem about themselves. Write your "I am" poem. As my own children would express themselves in writing, I could hear their inner voice and I could see the beginning stages of the development of passion and personality.

As parents and educators we have a responsibility to better understand the ways that we can make a difference in this on-going journey of personal development and growth. Asking the question what you see, how you feel, and what you think, connects us to the experience in front of us. It will have a greater impact on us. Being mindful of engaging all of our senses is relevant at any age.

Accessing Creative Capacities

We can change and access creative capacities by improving our environments and better understanding the brain and associative links to optimal development for children, teens, and young adults. We must manifest creativity in our daily lives. Creativity is all around us. We all should participate in some way. As a parent, there are ways to nurture your child's brain growth in ways that will enhance creativity.

Importance of Emotion

Emotional states affect the creative flow. When children are surrounded with positive emotion, nurturing environments, and on-going support, the mind tends to reach elevated states of happiness, joy and awe associated with more creativity. Even after the Kindergarten years, this could be through talking, reading, predicting, inquiring, exploring, pretending, experimenting, building, role-playing, and socializing.

Each child should grow and develop in a number of interrelated areas—social, emotional, communicative, cognitive, and physical. Invest in yourself. Being in a still, calm, and alert state of mind can carve a path. To attract what one wants, it is important to begin with creating a vision. When one clearly recognizes and connects emotionally and visually to their imagination, a vision can manifest, and one can deeply engage in creative thought. Each learner is curious, competent and able to take an active role in their own learning. By creating positive, innovative learning environments through sustaining rich, authentic relationships we can optimize potentials.

Early Childhood Education Report

Early Childhood Education Report (ECER) using benchmarks and evaluation of the quality of provincial/territorial early years services provides a comparison not only between provinces and territories every three years - 2011, 2014, 2017, 2020. Benchmark thresholds were influenced by those established by UNICEF in 2008 to promote the potential for continued international comparisons, and those included in the UNESCO 2010 cross-national study on the integration of early childhood education and care (Kaga, Bennett & Moss, 2010). Quebec had the largest percentage (73%) of 2-4 year olds regularly attending an ECE program, with

Ontario at 59% in 2017. The Northwest Territories, Yukon, British Columbia, Ontario, Quebec, Prince Edward Island, Nova Scotia, New Brunswick and Newfoundland all offer full-day kindergarten, meeting the needs of over 75% of the Canadian 5 year olds. Over the three year intervals an increasing trend of increased investment in early childhood education was evident. The updating the ECER 2020 research allowed me to examine the areas of growth and gaps that still existed.

Early Childhood Education Centre (ECEC) services have continued to develop in OECD countries, especially in Europe. The situation in Canada, however, has improved marginally since my previous research and examination of early childhood education released a decade ago. Childcare services in Canada are organized on a market model, resulting in unaffordable parent fees, inequitable and inadequate availability of services, and, too often, of low or modest quality (Beach and Ferns, 2015). What is required to address this crisis is already known.

For decades, childcare advocates, researchers, anti-poverty organizations, women's equality groups, Early Learning Child Care (ELCC) practitioners, and parents have been writing their side of the story. These stakeholders have developed a strong vision for a national system of universal, affordable, comprehensive, inclusive, and high-quality ELCC. According to the multinational assessment a system of universal, affordable, comprehensive, inclusive, and high-quality ELCC would:

- Enhance women's equality
- Support child development, including school readiness and wellbeing

- Help reduce poverty
- Ensure family-work balance
- Strengthen social integration and inclusion
- Alleviate the struggles of vulnerable children and families
- Foster economic prosperity

Globalization and the new economy demand the ability to learn and function as part of increasingly diverse groups. In a rapidly changing world, our knowledge of ourselves as individuals and group learners is equally important as absorbing information. Modern learners need to be flexible and responsive to changing needs. Working individually or collaboratively, digital literacy, distance learning, social media and coding also present an environment for creative thinking, broadening our local learning to a global platform. Educators and parents continue to inspire learners to be active, critically engaged, and continue to advocate for a brighter future and improved educational system. We all can continue to embrace new possibilities and opportunities through play and further curiosity and creativity.

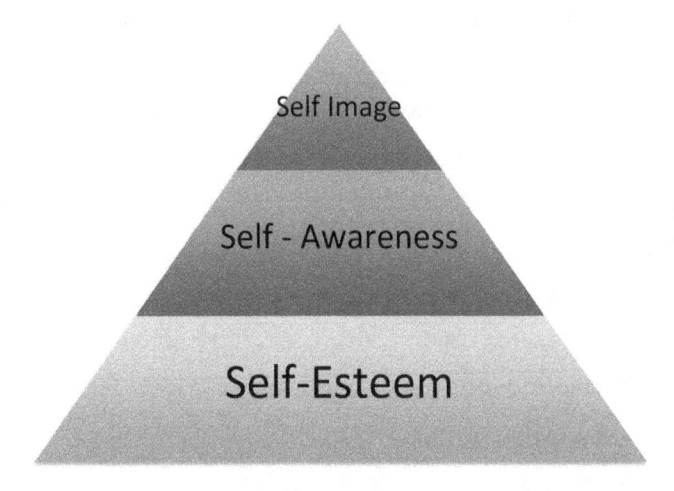

Figure 7: **Self-Development Model**

The Voice in the Head

Promoting approaches that allow both discovery of the outer and inner world during these times move us forward. Figuring out who they are and what underlying qualities reside inside them is a process of self-discovery. Students can be advancers, equalizers, connectors, or innovators. Based on their highest values a student can demonstrate and discover distinct interests. Specific patterns of behaviour and engagement can be revealed in students. Defining likes and dislikes can help foster interests and passions. Getting involved, reading, researching, and participating in activities that are areas of interest throughout all developmental stages foster growth and deeper awareness of oneself. Find the voice in your head.

In 2020 in schools we explored anti-racism at a new level. Unravelling and dismantling ideas of the how the colour of our skin means so much more than we think and significantly matters to identity. Instead of conforming and accepting we are all one we realized we are all so uniquely and truly different. There were expressions from students that there was discomfort in the skin students they were in. It was time to listen to the voice in their head. At times it could lead to bullying they said. The unfairness, the inequities, the barriers students faced had to be re-examined. As teachers we focused our professional development on learning, understanding, and making change happen.

By creating equitable inclusive spaces to meet the needs and honour all students. We had to dig a little deeper to feel the discomfort, shame and understand how students felt and were treated. As an educator it was important to build self-esteem, self-awareness and a positive self-image amongst students. Writing a guide for the inclusion of special needs children in the classroom provided a platform to build strategies, accommodation and modifications for learners to meet the needs of students. This is what was needed at the moment. See the world through someone else's eyes. Allowing time to create a space and lens to open new approaches, activities and resources to address these concerns became a priority. For educators, parents and students – your point of view of the world is shaped by your experience and is therefore highly biased towards your point of view and can limit future growth. Lets transform you monocular vision.

Rewire your brain to binocular vision by building self-value. Establish an internal mechanism of raising your self-value when it drops precipitously. Think about the most important things about you, feel the love towards important people in your life, image something beautiful in nature, listen to your favourite song. Let emotional intensity of negative thoughts vanish. Looking back and reflecting on historical events or situations and its impact on you can increase awareness of who you are as a person. Where were you before? Where are you now? Where do you wish to be? Take time to write poetry. My inspirational moments created a space for voice and I share a couple poems I wrote. It is a way to express myself - my thoughts, ideas and personal feelings.

CHAPTER 6

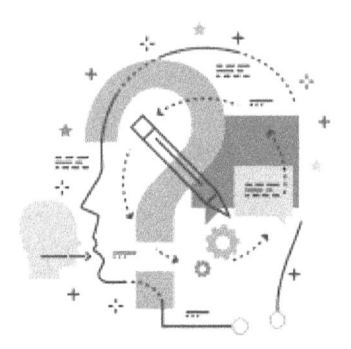

Inquiry

Explore and engage in your curiosities.

-E.Karia

Inquiry-based learning is fundamental for the development of higher order thinking skills. Vygotsky (1934), Dewey (1938), Piaget (1962), and Bruner (1961) advocated for discovery learning and demonstrated an understanding that open inquiry motivated student learning. Furthermore, Banchi and Bell (2008) explained that teachers should begin their inquiry instruction at the lower levels and work their way to open inquiry in order to effectively develop students' inquiry skills. Open inquiry activities are only successful if students are intrinsically motivated and if they are equipped with the skills to conduct their own research study. Inquiry-based learning is fundamental for the development of thinking skills. Lets examine the research on the importance of our environment and nature in learning. As an Educational Consultant engaging and counselling youth provided a pathway to blend research, resources and real-life adventures of students of diverse backgrounds.

Natural Curiosity

In the book, *Natural Curiosities: Building Children's Understanding of the World*, environmental inquiry as a pedagogical framework was developed by the Dr. Eric Jackman Institute of Child Study at the University of Toronto (The Laboratory School at the Dr. Eric Jackman Institute for Child Study, 2011). Teachers interviewed for this research study were aware of this resource, as it guided practice in their classroom. Environmental inquiry as a pedagogical approach was discussed. Through my meta-analysis and empirical evidence in early years studies conceptual components of creativity were linked to curiosity and inquiry.

Understanding the Importance of Environmental Education

According to UNESCO (1978) in the Tbilisi Declaration, environmental education is a learning process that increases people's knowledge and awareness about the environment and associated challenges. This helps individuals develop the necessary skills and expertise to address the challenges, and fosters attitudes, motivations, and commitments to make informed decisions and take responsible action. The roots of environmental education can be traced back as early as the 18th century. Jean-Jacques Rousseau (1979) stressed the importance of an education that focuses on the environment, the understanding that humans are good by nature, and the notion that learning should focus on emotion, not reason, in early years. Rousseau also believed that children should be raised close to nature and not in the city. Louis Agassiz, a Swiss-born naturalist, echoed Rousseau's philosophy as he encouraged students to "study nature, not books." These two influential scholars helped lay the foundation for a concrete environmental education program, known as 'nature study,' which took place in the late 19th century and early 20th century. Implications from my research suggested outdoor learning and play was beneficial to discovery and imaginative thinking.

Environmental Awareness

J. A. Palmer (1998), in the book *Environmental Education in the twenty-first Century: Theory, Practice, Progress and Promise*, shares a model for ecological thinking in which she defines the development of environmental understanding, awareness, and concern as well as which action needs to be developed in the Kindergarten years. Educational philosophies of Reggio Emilia, Waldorf, and Maria Montessori also encourage the integration of environmental education awareness and outdoor play in their program. Gardening, inquiry, and experiential learning connect with environmental education. As discussed in this study, connecting to nature in the early years is important for whole child development and was emphasized in many different educational philosophies as it is an integral part of child and brain development. Time outdoors for the children I observed provided hours of connectivity, joy and engagement.

Aasen, Grindheim, and Waters (2009), and Nimmo and Hallett (2008) suggest that young children already have an orientation toward each other and the natural world; it is the responsibility of schools to strengthen and sustain this orientation. An important focus in early years education, particularly in Ontario Kindergartens, is helping young children develop a love and respect for nature, building play around natural materials and bringing the concept of the outdoor classroom into FDK programs.

Integrating the natural world into different subject areas is also possible. For example, the connections between literacy, literature, and nature is receiving increasing attention, even in the educational mainstream. *A Place for Wonder*, a recent book by Georgia Heard and Jennifer McDonough (2009), taps into the potential to enhance both the development of young children's writing skills and their sense of wonder about the natural world.

Outdoor Exploration

Heard and McDonough (2009) described how they established opportunities in a Kindergarten class for wondering and pondering about questions in nature. Gardening offers an opportunity for taking action in the local natural environment (Sauvé, 2005). Outdoor play and experiences brought a sense of awe and wonder different from indoor classroom learning.

David Orr (2004), ecologist and scholar, emphasizes in his

book, *Earth in Mind: On Education, Environment, and the Human Prospect,* that our ability to restore planet Earth rests primarily on the decisions we make about education. Orr (2004) further discusses environmental inquiry initiatives that build on four pillars: inquiry-based learning, integrated learning, experiential learning, and stewardship. Getting children to build a growing commitment to protect water, air, plants, and wildlife builds a sense of care and responsibility that is important.

Natural Curiosity highlights ways of building children's understanding of the world through environmental inquiry. Knowledge Building (KB) circles and discourse can be ways of engaging children. We must engage deeper with the natural environment and we have to connect with earth and its natural elements. There is no doubt that a natural ebb and flow holds power.

During the pandemic we have all been further exploring the outdoors. Being aware of the outdoor beauty brings much awe, inspiration and clarity. With more emphasis on learning and reflection that occurs with time in nature, educators are being more mindful of the whole child as well as the inner soul of a child. Child-centered approaches respect the natural tendencies and exuberance of young learners and give opportunities for children to grow and develop their natural curiosities as they fully engage in the learning.

Policy Framework for Environmental Education

In 2009, the Ontario Ministry of Education released a policy document, *Policy Framework for Environmental Education in Ontario Schools,* which emphasized fostering children's sense of connection to each other and to the natural world through active participation.

It holds within its pages the potential to transform schooling in Ontario from an approach that relegates place to the periphery, both the potential of place to engage children in learning, and the innate, undeniable value of place if we are to live sustainable, healthy lives. In this century, increased funding and resources from the government support environmental education efforts in schools. Our present investments in building environmental awareness from an early age will lead to long-term improvements in the future.

Active Stewardship

Studying habitats of animals and the life cycle of a plant, along with discussing local and global environmental concerns or projects, will build awareness of the world around us. Through active citizenship and stewardship, from a young age we can promote more awareness and make our students environmentally conscious individuals. Scientific inquiry is a great way to build curiosities, awe, and wonder. There is a greater awareness of how humans impact the environment, and the impact that the environment has on calming and centering humans.

Schools are not only involved with eco-friendly recycling activities, but like to build in more field trips to marshes, ponds, forests, and natural habitats. In addition, the creation of outdoor spaces for learning is a growing concept with the emergence of the outdoor classroom. There is a growing and deeper connection with our earth, nature, and the outdoor environment in integrative and comprehensive approaches.

Whole Child Education

Education practices include the need to understand the goals of whole-child education. With emphasis on play-based and creative learning, educators are being more mindful of the whole child. Child-centered approaches respect the natural tendencies and exuberance of young learners and give opportunities for children to grow and develop their natural curiosities as they fully engage in learning.

The cherished experience with my husband and children when we finally reached the base and later climbed to the mountain peak of Machu Picchu in Peru. I realized nature is not something separate from us. We easily blend with nature if we are open to receive what it has to offer. When we say that we have lost our connection to nature, we've really lost our connection to ourselves. Nature is us and we are nature. We can deeply connect if we wish to. Awe is an overwhelming feeling associated with vastness, wonder and reverence.

Inquiry-based Learning as an Integrated Approach

Inquiry-based learning is primarily a pedagogical method, developed during the discovery learning movement of the 1960s. The philosophy of inquiry-based learning finds its antecedents in constructivist learning theories, such as the work of Piaget (1962), Vygotsky (1934, 1978), Bruner (1961), and Dewey (1938). Inquiry-based learning emphasizes constructivist ideas such as knowledge being built from experience and process, especially socially based experiences. Under this premise, learning develops best in group situations, with field work, case studies, investigation and research. Progress and outcomes are generally assessed by how well people develop experimental, analytical, and questioning skills. Nature walks, field trips, and outdoor play experiences children spark curiosities about the environment. Children will explore questions they may have, look into different scenarios, or look at a specific problem. Although a teacher or facilitator may assist the process, the discoveries and interests of the children themselves primarily lead it.

Heather Banchi and Randy Bell (2008) suggest that there are four levels of inquiry-based learning in science education: i) confirmation inquiry, ii) structured inquiry, iii) guided inquiry, and iv) open inquiry. The progression seen from level one through four provides an excellent guide for how to scaffold inquiry-learning skills for your students. Each type of inquiry is unique and the definitions of the four levels of inquiry are outlined below.

Four Levels of Inquiry

According to Banchi and Bell (2008), the four levels of inquiry have a specific focus. In confirmation inquiry, students are provided with the question and procedure (method), where the results are known in advance, and confirmation of the results is the object of the inquiry. Confirmation inquiry is useful to reinforce a previously learned idea; to experience investigation processes; or to practice a specific inquiry skill, such as collecting and recording data. In structured inquiry, students are provided with the question, procedure and task; they generate an explanation that is supported by the evidence collected in the procedure through evaluating and analysing the data that they collect. In guided inquiry, students are provided with only the research question, and the task is to design the procedure and to test the question and the resulting explanations. Because this kind of inquiry is more open than a confirmation or structured inquiry, it is most successful when people have had numerous opportunities to learn and practice different ways to plan experiments and record data. In open inquiry, students form questions, design procedures for carrying out an inquiry, and communicate their findings and results. This type of inquiry is often seen in science fair contexts where students drive their own investigative questions. In the Kindergarten classroom, the level of inquiry most often employed is guided inquiry. Beyond the Kindergarten years, inquiry learning allows students to seek knowledge through questions - it is both a practical and cognitive approach. They can hypothesize, explore, and investigate using their own inquisitive nature. An important part of inquiry is imagination. Using an unconventional way of looking at patterns that may not be obvious to adults, children incorporate plenty of new ideas and thoughts. Children can be passionately curious. Using the process of scientific inquiry, they are in a continual flight of wonder.

Play as a Vehicle for Engagement

Play is important for enhancing creativity. Play allows one to discover why and how things are done within a certain framework. This lends itself to finding new and different experiential solutions. Through creative play, young minds can grow emotionally, socially, intellectually, and even physically. Creative experiences help a student develop skills that will enable them to share their thoughts, feelings, and ideas. We are all born with the natural curiosity to learn, explore, and experiment. Children interact and fully engage with objects around, as they grow older, learning by creating is decreasing and this may be a bigger issue than we think. New connections and possible pathways build new knowledge. Developing predictability, visually, productivity, and originality develops intelligence. The interplay of curiosity, creativity, and play foster new ideas, a growth mind-set and ingenuity. Adaptability and flexibility also were part of creativity as it triggered divergent thinking and opportunities for idea generation.

Exploring High Vibration Emotions

With high vibrational emotions such as joy and bliss one enters a space of infinity and boundless opportunities while in a relaxed state of mind. In this stillness, one may be silent, yet have an intense amount of activity going on in their limbic system, frontal and parietal lobes, thalamus, and neural networks that are active. When a child is calm and comfortable they are more aware of what is going on inside and outside minds and their systems are subdued. It is when we have a monkey mind that we must focus our thoughts to be more productive with a deeper level of focus. There is a striking difference in brain waves between the two states. When a child is clear and focused, one sees slow, rhythmic alpha, theta, and gamma waves which are signs of deep relaxation. Creating spaces for children to find moments to experience the difference builds understanding of the meaning of calm. When the mind becomes still, one's intelligence explodes into new possibilities.

Goals in Education

There are three goals of education that must be addressed if we are to provide children with all that they need. First, we have to attend to children's academic achievement by providing them with an education that will ensure that they acquire the knowledge and skills necessary for success. Second, we must focus on the emotional and social as well as the cognitive domains if we are to serve the needs of the whole child. Third, we have to provide children with the means for learning so that they are able to connect with their outer and inner worlds. To realize these goals, we must provide a balance of the philosophies and develop integrated, innovative, and comprehensive practices that allow access to full, optimal, and multidimensional experiences.

There is clear evidence of shifts in educational practice as research reviews proven theories and explores experimentation and discovery of new innovative approaches. Classrooms using expansive approaches and newly designed spaces are becoming more open to novel insights. There is action, interaction, and reaction from pedagogists. Teachers, like children, feel the need to grow in their competencies. Teachers as researchers, facilitators, and active change agents can redesign and build an educational climate that aims to enhance children's development, to nourish and sustain, grow and satisfy desires for creativity, social interaction, language development, and exploration. Working collaboratively, researchers and teachers can continue to study children, their brain development and how they learn, research best teaching practices, and advocate for continued improvements, increase funding and support for quality educational programs. When we compare globally even access and quality of education we see that there is room for improvement.

New Science of Child Development: Parent Engagement

During the research observations of parents as partners in play, there was evidence of positive engagement and interactions with care-givers and children as they were emotionally excited and happy to share their learning. Different types of play facilitate and engage cognitive flexibility, emotional intelligence, and critical analysis. Parents participated in free play, inquiry play, collaborative play, and playful learning with provocations and invitations parents observed how learning happens. Educating parents through pedagogical documentation, open houses, parent teacher conferencing also added value. The new science of child development is examining the importance of the relationship between the parents and the children.

Engaging parents in school life yields many positive benefits leveraging home-school partnerships. Involved learning at home and at school is in the best interest of the child. Parents described ways in which their child expressed creativity. They said children were using more imagination in play, more creativity in their story-telling, varying their voice with facial expressions, and using varieties of sounds with their voice. Students learned collaboration and teamwork skills as they engaged in games and activities while enhancing communication and social skills.

Schooling and Learning

Makerspace stations for all ages, from Kindergarten to Grade 5, can be tremendously rewarding. Consideration of soft entry and planning soft transitions keeps children in a more relaxed state and allows for differentiated learning opportunities to better meet the needs of learners. A variety of materials such as coloured papers, coloured play doh, different sized cardboard boxes, recyclable containers, tape and yarn encouraged building three dimensional structures. Tinkering stations, weaving activities, shapes sorting, block play, gluing popsicle sticks refined fine motor skills. Exploring construction using container / cup towers, magnetic tools, nail and hammering station provided interesting materials to work such as wood, and metal.

Learning life skills by cooking, watering plants, gardening or using the sewing stations taught many preliminary useful household experiences. The use of loose parts provided open-ended mosaic art possibilities interest students. Often in different grade levels using soft entry with loose parts allowed a good transition before a subject lesson was taught. Question cards and challenges interest students. A green screen provided interesting learning opportunities. STEAM (Science, Technology, Engineering, Arts, and Math) experiences provided discovery learning opportunities with hands-on activities teaching math, technology, coding and science skills. Using natural elements (soils, sand, rocks, sticks, pine-cones and leaves) provided textured and sensory materials that could be stimulating and interesting to many children. There were several options to plan activities and as an educator you also learned to be creative in lesson planning. There are various online resources listed in *Appendix 5* to get students using technological resources at different ages groups to enhance learning experiences at any time.

In general, when we keep our core strong and allow it to be the basis of our practice, we are building a strong foundation and stronger partner relationships to gain a better understanding of our learners. Seeing, listening, we receive and use a lens to learn, but fully using all senses, interpreting and relating learning can advance to another level. It is this spiritual domain that defines the uniqueness of each individual; it deepens understanding of the inner being, thoughts, opinions, morals, and values.

Education builds Self-Awareness

The primary value of education and play lies in their contribution to self-awareness. Play can also help children discover their true selves, albeit in a more implicit manner. First, it provides children with the confidence needed to acquire self-esteem. Second, play facilitates a child's self-awareness. Through observing play, teachers can learn to care for children, to be mindful, and enhance their own self-awareness.

There is no other time in human development when so much can be learned in so brief a period. The period from 3.8 to 6 years old constitutes truly fanatically formative years, marked by intellectual growth, rapid development of motor skills, increased social maturity, and emotional self-regulation. As a teacher, profound moments of awe, wonder, and joy. They often left an impression. With a renewed and heightened personal constructivist approach in learning one could be more mindful of the child and trust and follow their lead. A nurturing environment, with indoor and outdoor spaces, where children can explore, play, and learn in the early years will give them the best possible start in their lives.

As an educator, I feel the need to connect, thrive, and accelerate innovative teaching practices to build happiness, resilience and self-care. It is a time to embody, absorb the transforming paradigm, and empower with innovation, creation and imagination. It is the spark that can awaken joy in creative expression and knowledge.

Fine Tuning Your Antennae

Building intentional kindness can go a long way. Practicing gratitude generates happy feelings. Gratitude can be with a daily written journal, a few moments each day to think of three good things that day. From a young age, children express appreciation and aspirations. Putting our minds at ease and becoming more relaxed may lead us on a journey of generosity of spirit. Self-kindness builds a positive state of being and stronger relationships that make us feel connected to others. We are never too young or old to fine tune our antenna. Sustaining compassion and empathy drive us in life. With better awareness of what can make us happy, there is increased productivity, better self-regulation, and space for increased creativity. Use creativity as an avenue to build empathy and compassion.

What are innovators?

Innovators are conscious children and know how to live in the moment. They connect with the present, and flourish from within. It is the power of educators to know why this learning, for this child, in this way, is important at this time. A nurturing environment, with indoor and outdoor spaces, where children can explore, play, and learn will give them the best possible start in their lives. It is the time for educators to be awakened to the need to connect, thrive and accelerate innovative teaching practices. In order to support the development of children, we also need to do a better job of supporting families and involving parents.

Making Tomorrow Better

It is a time to embody, and absorb the transforming paradigm. Empower oneself with innovation, creation and imagination. As partners in providing the best possible experiences and developmental opportunities for our next generation, educators, parents, policy-makers, researchers, and peers are all stakeholders, influencers and leaders in change. Let us continue to seek, share knowledge and accelerate what is needed to empower our youth for 21st century skills that will make children succeed and build a solid foundation for productive lives. The student's ability to see things differently, think divergently and solve problems, design and synthesize is evident in the classroom.

The Brain is the Foundation of the Human Mind

There is a compelling trans-disciplinary approach to understanding human development. Scientists have made advances in understanding brain development. As neurons fire together, they wire together. The inextricable role of our biology and how we think, learn, socialize, and behave emphasizes the importance of building brain architecture and brain pathways right from early development. The brain is the foundation of the human mind.

Bringing the science of early human development to the attention of policy makers and the public continues to increase awareness, evidence, investment, and support for quality educational experiences that each and every child deserves. Think above and beyond normal activities. Experience fresh new perspectives and perceive new meanings, and merge these with a background of familiar experiences. Let's continue to let our children thrive in the early years and beyond. Our past, present and future are a part of who we are. Taking time to reflect on these aspects brings awareness to our subconscious mind and deepens our understanding of concepts that interest us. An individual can nurture a passion, enhance skills and teach new methodologies or approaches for familiar subject matter. Accessing tools such as meditation can lead you on a path of self-discovery.

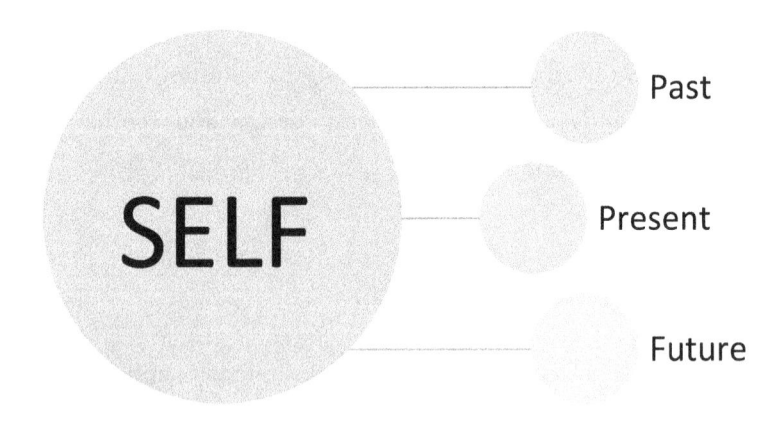

Figure 8: **Self-Development**

CHAPTER 7

Connectivity

*We are connected. People, trees, animals. Everything.
Seek Wholeness and Unity.*

- E. Karia

Play is important for enhancing creativity. It allows one to discover why and how things are done within a certain framework. It also lends itself to finding new and different solutions. As the world is changing so quickly and access to online information and online learning is becoming easier. Through creative play young minds can grow emotionally, socially, intellectually and even physically. Creative experiences help a student develop skills that will enable them to share their thoughts, feelings and ideas. We are all born with the natural curiosity to learn, explore and experiment. Children interact and fully engage with objects around them, however as they grow older, learning by creating is decreasing and this may be a bigger issue than we think. New connections and possible pathways build new knowledge. Developing predictability, productivity and originality develops intelligence. The interplay of curiosity, creativity and play foster new ideas, a growth mind-set and ingenuity.

The EYE Model as the "I" Model

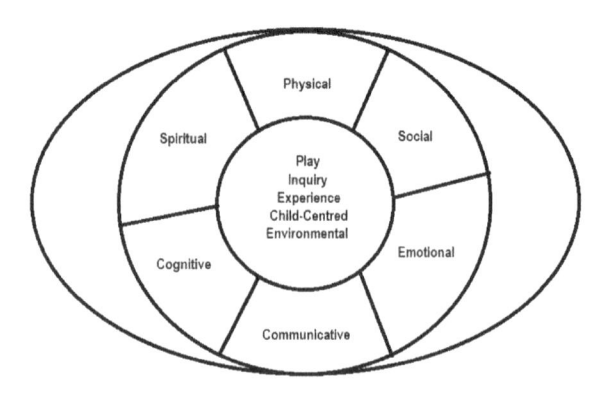

Figure 9: 'I' – Model – Finding Who Am I?

The EYE (Early Years Education) Model was originally developed to highlight the value of play experiences for holistic child development. Looking at Play, Inquiry, Experiential Learning, Child-Focused and Exploratory experiences add value to the learning engagements in Kindergarten years. Beyond the early years these approaches may continue to add value to student's educational experiences. Pedagogical shifts are evident beyond the Kindergarten years. Making the EYE Model empowering to the modern learner in grades above. A journey of self-discovery - we can now refer to the model as "The - I - Model" as it encourages tuning into domains of development, the inner spirit, and while building personal self beyond the early years.

Qualities that make someone special can be called their *x-factor*. We all have it and need to discover what it exactly is. Identifying your *x-factor* through broadening the depth and breadth of learning experiences and looking closer at self-awareness, personal identities and uniqueness may help reveal qualities, interests, and the whole self. Empowering students to connect with their unique self can allow them to embrace new truths and be open to different people, different perspectives which support inclusivity. Looking at various aspects of oneself - physical well-being, mental well-being, emotional stability, spiritual growth, cognitive abilities, and ability to communicate and express oneself directs one to look at their personal strengths and areas of growth. Self-reflection and introspection by looking into the mirror and identifying with who you see can reveal many self-impressions and may provide insight. Using the *I - Model* as a tool is useful to gain a holistic perspective of one's SELF.

```
                    /\
                   /  \
                  / Self-Actualization \
                 / individuality, uniqueness ☆ \
                /------------------------------\
               /  Self-esteem                   \
              /   - achievement, confidence  ☀  \
             /------------------------------------\
            / Social Needs - community, friends, school ☻ \
           /------------------------------------------------\
          /  Safety Needs - family, love, support    ♥       \
         /----------------------------------------------------\
        /  Basic Needs - food, shelter, sleep       ⌂          \
       /--------------------------------------------------------\
```

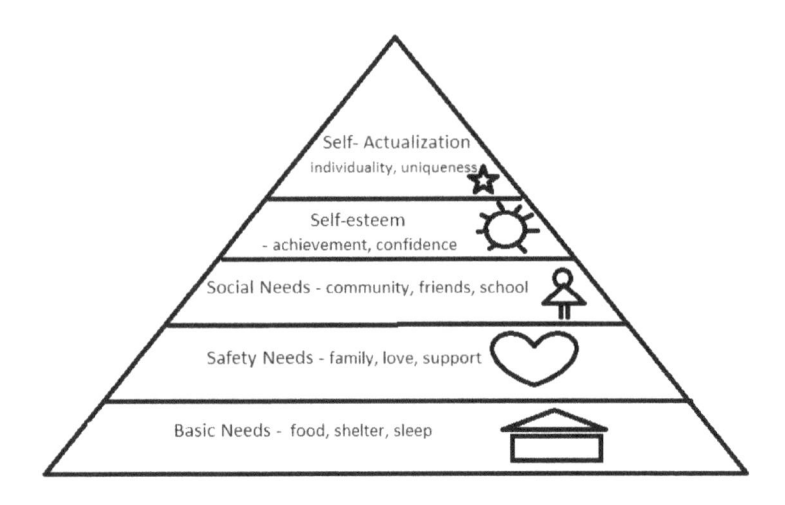

Figure 10: Maslow's Hierarchy of Needs - Understanding Child Development

Maslow's Hierarchy of Needs

Looking at Maslow's Hierarchy of Needs sheds light on human development. Psychologist Abraham Maslow (1943) defined a theory that showed stages of developing personal growth. Children need a variety of different experiences to facilitate this development. As growth is nurtured, the speed of processing, memory, and problem solving is strengthened. The pyramid model outlines specific needs of individuals from basic needs such as food, shelter and sleep. Love, family and social relationships support a sense of belonging, self-esteem and confidence. The top of the model is self-actualization and is a drive for creativity, morality and problem-solving.

By connecting deeply in learning children link to domains of child development such as physiological, socio-emotional, cognitive, communicative, physical, and spiritual needs of a child. Elements of play bridge children to friendships, community, and the world around them. The absence of play deprives the child of healthy development and learning.

Understanding Metaneeds

Maslow (1971) also coined a term, 'metaneeds' for the growth and nurturing of imagination and creativity. 'Metaneeds' includes: wholeness (unity), perfection (harmony and balance), completion (ending), justice (fairness), richness (complexity), simplicity (essence), liveliness (spontaneity), beauty (rightness), goodness (benevolence), uniqueness (individuality), playfulness (ease) and truth (reality) and meaningfulness (values). Connected with each of the levels in the Maslow's hierarchy are energy levels. Once thoughts, emotions and energies are aligned one's ability to create and manifest naturally flows.

Psychologist Abraham Maslow (1943) defined a theory that showed stages of developing personality and personal growth as a human. In his writings in *A Theory of Human Motivation in the Psychological Review*, Maslow (1943) illustrated what motivates human development and he defined it in a pyramid model (see *Figure 2*). The pyramid hierarchy outlines an order that shows—at the bottom—the specific needs of individuals, from basic needs such as food, shelter, and sleep that need to be met, then the need for safety and security. Love, family and social relationships are important in the social needs level and eventually the esteem level considers a sense of belonging, self-esteem, and confidence. Lastly, the top of the triangle is self-actualization needs or higher level needs such as the drive for creativity, morality, and problem-solving at the top tier.

Maslow defined levels distinguishing the more basic to more complex needs as one goes up the ladder. It is during certain ages even children have a desire to achieve and excel beyond the basic needs. While one may initially focus on the food, shelter and relationships they will move beyond these basic needs. One may eventually feel more inclined for intellectual achievement, higher-level thinking, engaging the brain and mind in greater potentials. This inner fire and light drives and motivates each student. Without this inner spark and this personal passion and drive to dig deeper, reach higher the paradigm of shifts and transformation would not occur. Students' personal visions and desires also explain a little more about human behaviour and being human as children mature and grow.

In the 1960s, Abraham Maslow conducted research about 'peak experiences' and 'ecstasy' and it is part of the power of awe. I've been struck with wonder on how peak experiences and awe can be found in everyday common places. We just have to keep our antennae up for the sense of wonder and awe that is everywhere. In early spring, when the daffodils and tulips bloom, I'm reminded that peak experiences can literally be found in our backyard. Finding those surreal moments when you almost have to pinch yourself to make sure you're not dreaming. Wonderment can bring feelings of unity, joy, eternity, calm, and perfection. For me being near water, mountains, trees, flowers, sunrise, or sunlight brings an ecstatic feeling.

Identifying Peak Experiences

Peak experiences are described by Maslow as "especially joyous and exciting moments in life, involving sudden feelings of intense happiness and well-being, wonder and awe, and possibly also involving an awareness of transcendental unity or knowledge of higher truth (as though perceiving the world from an altered, often vastly profound and awe-inspiring perspective).". Maslow argued peak experiences should continue to be studied and cultivated. They are "a route to personal growth, integration and fulfilment" For me the length of my walk in nature inspired the length of my writing. Hiking trails in Sedona, Arizona brought a heightened sense of peak experience. At the outset the degree of adventure made the whole landscape glow with enthusiasm, enchantment banishing a sense of time. The self-empowerment model in *Appendix 6* includes three levels of self-empowerment – build the base with self-esteem, self-awareness and then create self-image.

With high-energy emotions and zero limits one enters a space of infinity and boundless opportunities. In a space where a relaxed and feeling of calmness is an entirely different state. A child can be still and silent yet have an intense amount of activity going on in their limbic system, frontal and parietal lobes, thalamus and neural networks that are active when we have a monkey mind. When a child is calm and relaxed they are more aware of what is going on inside and outside minds and their systems are subdued. There is a striking difference in brain waves between the two states. When a child is calm one sees slow, rhythmic alpha, theta and gamma waves which are signs of deep relaxation. Creating spaces for children to find moments to experience the difference builds understanding of the meaning of calm. When the mind becomes still one's intelligence explodes into new possibilities.

Make Meditative Moments a Daily Practice

Close your eyes. Focus on your breath, inhale and exhale. When you inhale count to four and when you exhale count to four a few times to get you into a good calm space. Connect with your imagination by focusing on an area of the mind, the point between your eyebrows, just above your nose. Imagine a white light there. Other access points for your imagination can be your heart and head. Focus on your heart and imagine white light shining there. Then focus on the top of your head and visualize a white light coming in from the crown of your head. For concentration you can add a mantra as you inhale and exhale. Inhale 'peace' and exhale 'love' and say "I am peace, I am love, I am joy". Remember the universe is supporting you right now. Relax your entire body. Imagine the white light flowing all through your body and radiating throughout and radiating into the world and this circle of light will be carried with you as support around you all the time. You now feel lighter.

CHAPTER 8

Diversity

Knowing yourself is the beginning of all wisdom.

-Aristotle

You have many diverse dimensions. We are each capable and competent. Let's start by reflecting or journaling about yourself. Refining your distinctions begins with understanding your truth. What are some of your competent activities? Which are some of your incompetent activities? Classifying activities will help identify your strengths. Then identify your unique ability activities. This may highlight some of your passions and interests. Start to think about how you will invest time to grow your unique ability.

Diverse Dimensions in Education

There are three goals of education that must be addressed if we are to provide children with tools that will move them forward in their journey. First, we have to attend to children's academic achievement by providing them with an education that will ensure that they acquire the knowledge and skills necessary for success. Second, we must focus on the emotional and social as well as the cognitive domains if we are to serve the needs of the whole child. Third, we have to provide children with the means for learning so that they are able to connect with their outer and inner worlds. To realize these goals, we must provide a balance of the philosophies and develop integrated, innovative and comprehensive practices that allow access to full, optimal and multidimensional experiences.

There is clear evidence of shifts in educational practice, embarkation on leading edge research, review of proven theories and experimentation that nurture discovery. Classrooms have become wider and varied spaces using expansive approaches and becoming more open to novel insights. There is action, interaction and reaction from pedagogists. Teachers like children feel the need to grow in their competencies. Teachers as researchers, facilitators and active change agents can redesign and build an educational climate that aims to enhance children's development, to nourish and sustain, grow and satisfy desires for creativity, social interaction, language development, and exploration. Working collaboratively, educators can continue to study children, their brain development and how they learn, research best teaching practices, and advocate for continued improvements, increase funding and support for quality educational programs. When we compare globally even access and quality of education we see that there is room for improvement.

Importance of Parental Involvement

Establishing community connections added value to defining individuality. During the research observations of parents as partners in play there was evidence of positive engagement and interactions with care-givers and children and children felt emotionally excited and happy to share their learning. Different types of play facilitate and engage cognitive flexibility, emotional intelligence, and critical analysis. Parents participated in free play, inquiry play, collaborative play, and playful learning with provocations and invitations parents observed how learning happens. Educating parents through pedagogical documentation, open houses, parent teacher conferencing also added value. The way children interacted with other adults and children revealed much about their character.

Engaging parents in school life yields many positive benefits leveraging home-school partnerships. Involved learning at home and at school is in the best interest of the child. Parents described ways in which their child expressed creativity. They said children were using more imagination in play, became more creative in their story-telling, varying their voice with facial expressions and sound of voice, expressing interesting details in writing and sharing amazing ideas and extending those ideas. Students learned collaboration and teamwork skills as they engaged in games and activities along with communication and social skills.

Inspirations from Makerspace and STEAM

Makerspace stations for all ages from Kindergarten to Grade 5 can be tremendously rewarding. Consideration of soft entry and planning soft transitions keeps children in a more relaxed state and allows for differentiated learning opportunities to better meet the needs of learners. A variety of materials (paper, playdoh, cardboard boxes, recyclables), tinkering stations, weaving activities, shapes various colours sizes for block play, popsicle stick construction, container towers, magnetic tools, nail and hammering station, cooking or sewing stations teach many preliminary exploration experiences encouraging broader and more creative thinking. Use of loose parts provides open-ended mosaic art possibilities that interest students. Question cards and challenges interest students. A green screen provides an interesting learning space. STEAM (Science, Technology, Environmental, Arts and Math) strategies provide discovery learning opportunities with hands-on activities teaching math and engineering and science skills. Use of natural elements (rocks, sticks, pine-cones) provided varied textured materials. There are several ways to plan for valuable learning opportunities through STEAM.

Importance of the laying a Foundation

In general, when we keep our core strong and allow it to be the basis of our practice, we are building a strong foundation and stronger partner relationships to gain levels of perspectives and a better understanding of our learners. Seeing, listening we receive and use a lens to learn but fully using all senses, interpreting and relating learning can advance to another level. It is this spiritual domain that defines the uniqueness of each individual; it deepens understanding of the inner being, thoughts, opinions, morals, and values. The primary value of education and play lies in their contribution to self-awareness. Play can also help children discover their true selves, albeit in a more implicit manner. First, it provides children with the confidence needed to acquire self-esteem. Second, play facilitates a child's self-awareness. Through observing play, teachers can learn to care for children, to be mindful of them, and to enhance their own self-awareness.

Invest in the Early Years

There is no other time in human development when so much can be learned in so brief a period. The period from 3.8 to 6 years old constitutes truly fanatically formative years, marked by intellectual growth, rapid development of motor skills, increased social maturity, and emotional self-regulation. As a teacher there were many observations of profound moments of awe, wonder and joy. They often left an impression. With a renewed and heightened personal constructivist approach in learning one could be more mindful of the child and trust and follow their lead. A nurturing environment, with indoor and outdoor spaces, where children can explore, play, and learn in the early years will give them the best possible start in their lives. As an educator I feel the need to connect, thrive and accelerate innovative teaching practices to build happiness, resilience and self-care. It is a time to embody, absorb the transforming paradigm and empower with innovation, creation and imagination.

Design Your Destiny

Self-kindness builds a positive state of being and stronger relationships that make us feel connected to others. We are never too young or old to fine tune the most beautiful part of you. What do you look like when you are at your best? What things do you always do and Why? Finding your x-factor, your north star or your touchstone allows you to be your best self. Your uniqueness will always be with you growing and expanding. With better awareness there is increased productivity, better self-regulation and space opens up for increased creativity. Use creativity as an avenue to build empathy and compassion. Higher compassion and empathy feeds a higher purpose in life. Be an innovator and persevere, strive for connection, ask questions, make meaning, and think creativity in many aspects of your life.

EXPLORING CREATIVITY

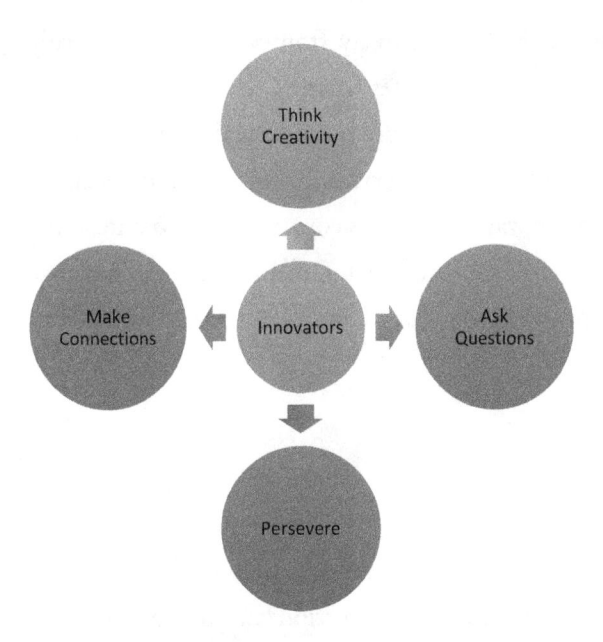

Figure 11: **Qualities of Innovators**

Construct, Collaborate and Challenge

Innovators are conscious children that know how to live in the moment, connect with the present, and flourish from within. It is the power of educators to know why this learning, for this child, in this way is important at this time. A nurturing environment, with indoor and outdoor spaces, where children can explore, play, and learn will give them the best possible start in their lives. It is the time for educators to be awakened to the need to connect, thrive and accelerate innovative teaching practices. In order to support the development of children we also need to do a better job of supporting families and involving parents. Working towards being a transparent and effective communicator allows you to be more open, honest and speak freely from your heart. Be truly genuine and this authenticity creates trusting relationships that will nurture your growth. Create paradigms and breakthroughs to a bigger and better future by accessing existing structures and systems to support you along the way. Innovators construct, collaborate and challenge. Using these 3 C's – Construct, Collaborate and Challenge any idea or concept can be developed and redesigned. Be the flame lighting other fires.

Making Tomorrow Better

It is a time to embody, absorb the transforming paradigm and empower with innovation, creation and imagination. As partners in providing the best possible experiences and developmental opportunities for our next generation educators, parents, policy-makers, researchers and peers are all stakeholders, influencers and leaders in change. Let us continue to seek, share knowledge and accelerate what is needed to empower our youth for 21st century skills that will make children succeed and build a solid foundation for productive lives. Having the ability to see things differently, think divergently and solve problems, design and synthesize.

There is a compelling trans-disciplinary approach to understanding human development. Scientists have made advances in understanding brain development. As neurons fire together they wire together. The inextricable role of our biology and how we think, learn, socialize and behave emphasizes the importance of building brain architecture and brain pathways right from early development. The brain is the foundation of the human mind. Bringing the science of early human development to the attention of policy makers and the public continues to increase awareness, evidence, investment and support for quality educational experiences that each and every child deserves. Think above and beyond normal activities and strive to explore creativity. It is beyond expression in artwork to boundless forms and ways of showing or knowing - find your way to express it. With a focus on transformational education with elements of creativity, curiosity, inquiry, connectivity and diversity we can move in a new paradigm of self-identity as we meet the needs of our students for 21st century learning needs.

Neurogenesis, or the process by which neurons are produced from stem cells in adults has been recently studied and continues to be of interest. Can adults continue to develop brain cells? It has shown that meditation can support neurogenesis by increasing grey matter density. Going back to the *Self-Empowerment Kit* we need to establish values, be mindful, learn to self-regulate, take time for meditative moments and establish emotional presence. This toolkit can begin your journey of self-discovery. Building our self-value by thinking about the components of the *Self-Empowerment Model* remind us to build self-esteem, self-awareness and our self-image. Continue to be a life-long learner!

Conclusion

Experience fresh new perspectives and perceive new meanings, as you merge these ideas with a background of familiar experiences. This will begin to empower you. Let's continue to let our children thrive in the early years and beyond. They will synthesize and make meaning in shared meaning in the relationships they engage in with others, self and the world surrounding them. By visualizing creative ideas and designing solutions we all can attract what is needed to streamline the process and achieve the results desired. Gain fundamental self-knowledge to define who you truly are. Identify and believe in your talent to develop your amazing potential. Make every fragrance of self-talk a little story in your head that will make your dream a reality. Be your own advocate and driving force to move forward. Each day the sun shines to remind you of eternal life, the skies speak silently reminding you of your soul's inner guidance. May you always be surrounded by Mother Nature's sweet embrace and be inspired by its sacred wisdom. Walk in wonder, inhale the bouquet that lies before you, feel the earth beneath your feet and allow yourself to be thoroughly grounded in the knowledge of your place in this universe.

I am Grateful

Today and everyday,
I'm grateful.
For the sunrise and sunset.
For the forest full of trees,
The animals, the birds,
The lakes, rivers and seas,
I'm grateful for all the inspirations,
I'm grateful for the love that binds us and the wind that sometimes knocks us off our feet. The warmth of the sun, the mystery of the moon and coolness of a breeze.
As I have grown I have gained knowledge, continued learning and opened my wings. Like a caterpillar turning into a butterfly I thrive and transform.
In uncertain times, I feel the need to accelerate my inner search. To be heard.
Gathering thought, communicating feelings, expressing myself better each day.
I'm grateful for all those who helped me understand.

I am

Today and everyday,
I promise to continue to take time to
understand the beauty of unique souls.
Gifts that continue to shape our world and offer so much to us.
Each soul has a unique purpose! Each one is special!
Each one is empowered!

Today and every single day.
I stand, I am
I am human
I am woman
I am curious
I am creative
I am learning
I am happy
I am me

APPENDIX 1

The Emotional Wheel – Build Self-Awareness with Emotional Presence

Simply observing your child's feelings and accepting them teaches children to identify emotions in themselves and others. As you go through your day, look for opportunities to acknowledge feelings. One can use the **wheel** to identify their **emotions** and come to terms to how they are feeling and, ultimately, become more self-aware and self-compassionate. This is a pathway to inner self and self-discovery.

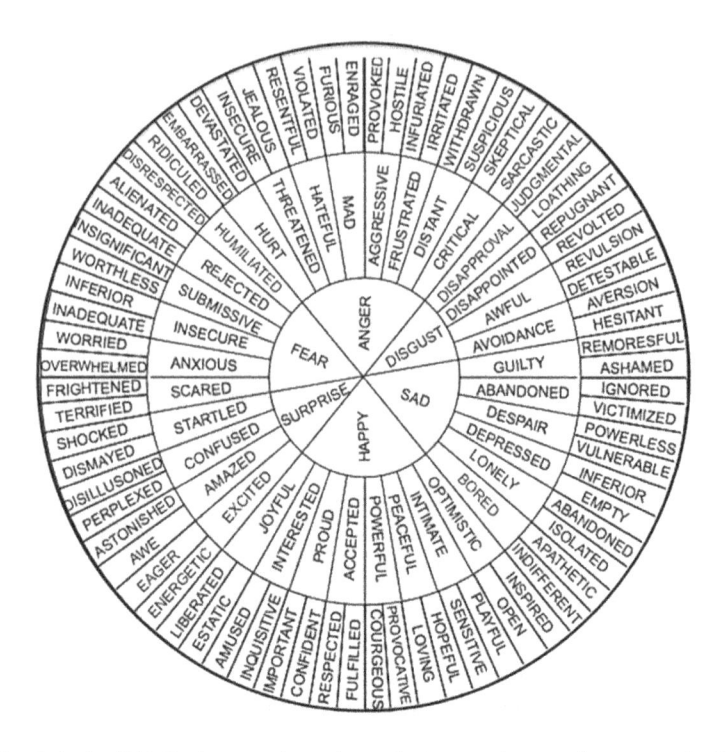

Plutchik, R. (1980). A general psychoevolutionary theory of emotion. In R. Plutchik & H. Kellerman (Eds.), Emotion: Theory, research and experience, Theories of emotion (Vol. 1, pp. 3–33). New York: Academic Press

APPENDIX 2

Tips for Parents

As a parent and educator I often was conscious of this need and continued to figure out ways to nurture this journey. Here are some ideas that may help to cultivate creativity. Things I may have discovered along the way.

Fostering Creativity for Children:

- design a space for creativity
- allow for 'free time' and 'free thinking'
- giving access to a variety of loose parts (e.g. tubes, sticks, rocks, gems, etc.)
- engaging with a variety of medium and materials
- connecting at a deeper level with what interests an individual
- variety of block play experiences using different materials
- painting giving opportunities to mix and use of various colours
- allowing for imaginative play

- activate a child's senses
- allow opportunities to problem-solve
- avoid over parenting and over managing
- let them get messy
- allow children to play in sand and water, explore bubbles and play dough
- let them make mistakes as they are opportunities for growth
- minimize screen time
- let them share their story
- encourage creative solutions
- make the visual space a reflection of creative learning space
- have a sketchbook
- use apps that allow graphic design
- use iPad as a tool to enhance creativity (e.g. photography, videography, etc.)
- make new things with the same materials (e.g. a box of paper clips on a desk)
- experiment with cooking / baking with children by changing an ingredient
- gather materials and present a challenge
- observe and then facilitate creative thinking by asking questions
- offering support to children - 'What can I do to help you?"
- really understand what they are thinking, feeling and seeing
- genuinely see what they are interested in at that moment

APPENDIX 3

Tips for Students

Empowering Teenagers with mindfulness activities:

- add exercises to your daily routine
- don't dabble - do things in depth
- practice meditation, mindfulness and deep breathing
- make time for 'just thinking' or 'just feelings'
- dissociate from any kind of input from outside world
- find moments to just sit and be silent and still
- let your mind wander, float and think freely to create novel associations
- take walks in nature and the outdoor environment is great space for inspiration
- choose a topic to explore and study / observe it for a month (e.g. birds, trees)
- observe aspects you may not have normally noticed
- exercise emotional and intellectual components
- be aware of emotional associations and feelings you experience with certain things

- what thoughts of feeling does a particular object/person evoke
- describe orally or in writing what you observe
- discuss in detail your experience - choosing perfect words
- build on descriptions using visual thought, words, writing and drawings on paper
- notice as you change a topic each month if you are getting better and better
- observing in an intuitive and analytical manner becomes habitual
- do the 'observe people' exercise to better remember names and people
- practice imagining - be anyone or anything anywhere or any place
- expand personal perspectives of the world so that you can be liberated
- tackle new fields you know little about
- choose new interests to broaden thinking

General Tips:

- allow unique perspectives and honour individuals to pursue their interests
- leverage strengths and let them engage deeply and build long-term passions
- be aware of what they like and don't like - take a moment to reflect on this
- understand who they are and what they are about - listen, observe, analyse

- be fully present and mindful - listen, engage, dialogue and interact genuinely
- design and create a special space for creative exploration in your home
- stay deeply connected with people and observe them grow and evolve

APPENDIX 4

Creating Creative Learning Spaces

1. How can I bring more creativity into a child's life? Throughout the day?
2. How can I enhance imaginative play experiences?
3. What are the different materials and loose parts to introduce to children?
4. How can the environment encourage choice and excite children to learn?
5. Am I facilitating opportunities to think, ponder and engage deeply?
6. Is the child building on natural curiosities and leading the inquiry?
7. Does the learning experience go beyond intelligence and rekindle enthusiasm?
8. Does the learning nurture a student's personal confidence and self-esteem?

9. Are there learning experiences to share ideas and encourage dialogue?
10. Can the learning experience be extended in different ways at different levels?
11. How can educators strengthen learning partnerships with all stakeholders?
12. What are some ways to professionally manage conflicts and difference of opinions?
13. How can the relationship with families be more meaningful and supportive?
14. Does our questioning respect student thinking and enhance the learning?
15. How can we change the environment to reduce the children's stress levels?
16. Are there different ways to keep children calm, alert and engaged in learning?
17. How can learning partners co-construct and collaborate in better ways?
18. Can we make mundane tasks more interesting, and provide smoother transitions?
19. Have we been organic in the flow of the day, being mindful that each day is different?
20. Is this learning, for this child, in this way, most engaging at this time?

APPENDIX 5

On-Line Resources for Learning

Below is a list of on-line educational resources useful to learners, educators and parents to educate, engage and empower children and youth both at home and school. Any comments or inquiries regarding the linked web sites should be directed to the host organization.

Name of Resource	Description	Early Years K-2	Primary Grades 1-3	Junior Grades 4-6
GONoodle	Fun and creative ways to help get students moving.	✓	✓	✓
Visual Arts	This activity is ideal for any age, inspired by ordinary objects and your imagination. See how many ideas you can come up with and make a story from them.	✓	✓	✓

Music	Free virtual instruments online.	✓	✓	✓
G Major Music Theory	Free resource for students with keyboards to practice their skills, view demos and learn theory.			✓
Draw Everyday with JJK	A Youtube Channel featuring daily drawing classes with illustrator, Jarret Krosoczka	✓	✓	✓
Lunch Doodles with Mo Willams	Youtube Channel featuring daily drawing activities and writing process inspiration.	✓	✓	✓
MediaSmarts	A variety of tutorials, games and articles focused on digital citizenship, media literacy and current digital issues.		✓	✓
Language bit.ly/bringthellchome	A variety of activities to do with your children. An example is have Robert Munsch read the Paper Bag Princess then do some follow up activities. Some involve technology, others research. Click on the various icons for a variety of activities. There are three grids: story time, maker and collections where you have some starting points for various activities.	✓	✓	✓

International Children's Library http://en.childrenslibrary.org/	Lots of different options for various reading levels and many different languages also. You can search by age, characters and much more.	✓	✓	✓
Read Alouds https://www.storylineonline.net	This is a website where actors read books aloud for students to enjoy.	✓	✓	✓
Math https://www.tumblemath.com/autologin.aspx?U=tumble2020&P=A3b5c6	**TumbleMath** - K-6 math ebook database	✓	✓	✓
The Global Virtual Stock Exchange	A free Global Online Stock Game that allows participants to trade stocks, commodities, and currencies from several different countries from around the world.			✓
Crash Course Economics	A series of 35 videos that explain a variety of topics including supply and demand, specialization, trade, taxation, labour markets, game theory, etc.			✓

Everfi	A variety of course options related to business education: • Financial Literacy • Investing Basics • Entrepreneurial Expedition			✓
Scratch Jr.	A free app that teaches young children (ages 5-7) how to program their own interactive stories and games. Solve problems, design projects, and express themselves creatively on the computer	✓	✓	
Scratch	A free app that teaches young people how to program their own interactive stories and games. Think creatively, reason systematically, and work collaboratively.	✓	✓	
Code.org	Curriculum for K-6 computer science from simple apps to complex computer programs.	✓	✓	✓

APPENDIX 6

Self-Empowerment Model

Whether a student or educator we all can better learn who we truly are. Consider each level of development building a foundation and creating YOU! Be Your Most Empowered SELF. Access the Self-Empowerment Toolkit techniques in your journey. This will get you started and keep you grounded.

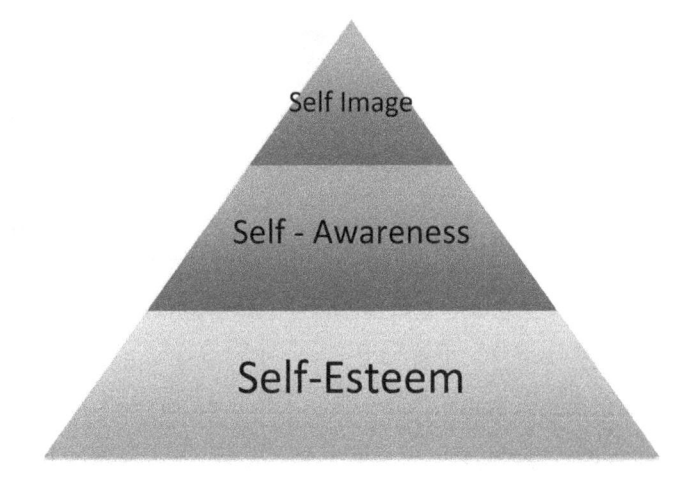

- Self Image
- Self - Awareness
- Self-Esteem

Try a Personal Survey

Go to www.viacharacter.org and complete the free survey. Explore the Enneagram Test online at http://www/eclecticenergies.com/enneagram/

REFERENCES

Best Start Expert Panel on Early Learning (2007). *Early learning for every child today: A framework for Ontario early childhood settings*. Toronto, Ontario: Ontario Ministry of Children and Youth Services.

Bergin, C., & Bergin, D. (2009). Attachment in the classroom. *Educational Psychology Review*, 21(2), 141-170.

Blair, C., & Diamond, A (2008). Biological processes in prevention and intervention: The promotion of self-regulation as a means of preventing school failure. Development and Psychopathology, 20 (3), 899-911.

Bogdan, R., & Biklen, S. K. (2006). *Qualitative research for education: An introduction to theories and methods*. Needam, MA: Allyn and Bacon.

Bredekamp, S. (Ed.). (1987). *Developmentally appropriate practice in early childhood programs serving children from birth through age 8*. Washington, DC: National

Bruner, J. (1996). *The Culture of Education*. Cambridge, MA: Harvard University Press

Bruner, J. (1961). The act of discovery. *Harvard Educational Review, 31*(1), 21-32.

Bruner, J. (1967). *On Knowing: Essays for the left hand*. Boston: Harvard University Press.

Bruner, J., Sylva, K., & Genova, P. (Eds.).(1976). *The role of play in the problem solving of children 3–5 years old*. New York: Basic Books.

Canadian Council on Learning. (1996, 2007). *Report on the state of early childhood learning*. Ottawa, Ontario: Canadian Council on Learning.

Canadian Council on Learning—Early Childhood Learning Knowledge Center. (2006). Let the children play: Nature's answer to early learning. In *Lessons in learning*. Ottawa, Ontario: Canadian Council on Learning.

Cleveland, G., Corter, C., Pelletier, J., Colley, S., Bertrand, J.,& Jamieson, J. (2006). *Early childhood learning and development in child care, Kindergarten and family support Programs*. Toronto, ON: Atkinson Center at OISE/UT.

Dewey, J., (1987). *My Pedagogic Creed*. First Published in *School Journal. 54, no. 3 (1897). 77-80.*

Dewey, J. (1938\1997). *Experience and education* (Original work published 1929 by New York, NY: Kappa Delta Pi). New York, NY: First Touchstone.

Dewey, J., (1934). *Art of Experience*: New York, NY: Perigee Books

Dewey, J. (1933). *How we think.* Boston: D.C. Heath.

Einstein, A. (1932). The world as I see it. In C. Seeling (Ed.). *Ideas and Opinions Based on Mein Weltbild* (pp. 8-11). NY: Bonanza Books, 1954.

Felver, J.C., Celis-de Hoyos, C.E., Tezanos, K., & Singh, N. N. (2016). *A Systematic Review of Mindfulness-Based Interventions for Youth in School Settings.* Mindfulness, 7(1), 34-45.

Fredrickson, B. L. (2001). The Role of Positive Emotions in Positive Psychology. *American Psychologist,* 56 (3), 218-226.

Froebel, F. (1887). *The education of man.* New York, NY: Appleton-Entury Crofts.

Gardner, H. (1983). *Multiple Intelligences: The theory in practice.* New York, NY: Basic Books

Gardner, H. (1987). Beyond IQ: Education and human development. *Harvard Educational Review,* 57(2), 187-193.

Goldberg, L.R. (1990). An alternative description of personality: The Big Five personality traits. *Journal of Personality and Social Psychology,* 59, 1216-1229.

Greenspan, S. & Shanker, S. (2004). *The first idea: How symbols, language and intelligence evolved from our primate ancestors to modern humans.* Cambridge, MA: Da Capo Press.

Huntsinger, J. (2013). Does Emotion Directly Tune the Scope of Attention? *Current Directions in Psychological Science,* 22(4), 265-270

Huttenlocher, P.R. (2002). *Neural plasticity: The effects of environment on the development of the cerebral cortex.* MA: Harvard University Press.

Kaga, Y., Bennett, J., & Moss, P. (2010). Caring and Learning Together: A Cross-National Study of Integration of Early Childhood Care and Education within Education. Paris: UNESCO.

Karia, E. (2015). *Fostering Creativity: The Full Day Kindergarten Classroom in Ontario: Learning through Inquiry and Play and its Implications for Child Development.* Bloomington, IN: iUniverse.

Lantieri, L. (2001). *Schools with spirit: Nurturing the inner lives of children and teachers.* Boston, MA: Beacon.

Legislative Assembly of Ontario. (2010). *Bill 242, Full-Day early learning statute law amendment act, 2010.* Retrieved from www.ontla.on.ca

Maattam, E., Mykkanen, A., & Jarvela, S. (2016). Elementary School Children's Self and Social Perceptions of Success. *Journal of Research in Childhood Education,* 30(2), 170-184.

Malaguzzi, L. (1993). For an education based on relationships. *Young Children, 49*(1), 9-12.

Maslow, A. (1943). A theory of human motivation. *Psychological Review, 50*(4), 370-96. Retrieved from http://psychclassics.yorku.ca/Maslow/motivation.htm

Maslow, A. (1954). *Motivation and personality.* New York, NY: Harper and Row.

Maslow, A. (1970). *Motivation and personality* (2nd Ed.). New York, NY: Harper and Row.

Maslow, A. (1971). *Farther Reaches of Human Nature.* New York, NY: McGraw-Hill.

McCain, M. N., & Mustard, J. F. (1999). *Reversing the real brain drain: Early years study.* Toronto, Ontario: Publications Ontario.

McCain, M. N., Mustard, J. F., & Shanker, S. (2007). *Early years study 2: Putting science into action.* Toronto, Ontario: Council for Early Child Development.

McCain, M. N., Mustard, J. F., & McCuaig, K. (2011). *Early years study 3: Making decisions: Taking action.* Toronto, Ontario: Margaret & Wallace McCain Family Foundation

McCrae, R.R. & John, O.P. (1992). An introduction to the five-factor model and its applications. *Journal of Personality, 60,* 175-215.

McCrae, R. R., & Costa, P.T. (1987). Validation of the five-factor model of personality across instruments and observers. *Journal of Personality and Social Psychology,* 52, 81-90.

McCuaig, K., Akbari, E., Foster, D., Plamondon, A., Karia, E., Soloway, A. & Hernandez, M (2019) *Early Learning and Childcare Innovation ToolKit.* Toronto, ON: Atkinson Centre for Society and Child Development, OISE/University of Toronto.

McCuaig K. & Akbari, E. (2017). *The early childhood education report 2017.* Toronto, ON: Atkinson Centre for Society and Child Development, OISE/University of Toronto.

Metz, S.M., Frank, J.L., Reibel, D., Cantrell, T., Sanders, R., & Broderick, P.C. (2013). *The Effectiveness of the Learning to BREATHE Program on Adolescent Emotion Regulation.* Research in Human Development, 10(3), 252-272.

Ministry of Children and Youth Services. (2006). *Ontario's best start action plan: A progress report.* Toronto, Ontario: Government of Ontario.

Mustard, J.F. (2006). *Early child development and experience-based brain development: The scientific underpinnings of the importance of early child development in a globalized world.* Washington, DC: Brookings Institute.

National Scientific Council on the Developing Child. (2007). *Young children develop in An environment of relationships.* Cambridge, MA: Harvard University Press.

Nimmo, J., & Hallett, B. (2008). Childhood in the garden: A place to encounter natural and social diversity. *Young Children, 63* (1), 32-38.

Ontario Ministry of Education (2003a). *Early reading strategy: The report of the experience panel on early reading in Ontario.* Retrieved from http://www.edu.gov.on.ca/eng/document/reports/reading/reading.pdf

Ontario Ministry of Education (2003b). *Early math strategy: The report of the expert panel on early math in Ontario.* Retrieved from http://www.edu.gov.on.ca/eng/document/reports/math/math.pdf

Ontario Early Years (2004). *Achieving cultural competence.* Toronto, Ontario: Ministry of Children and Youth Services.

Ontario Ministry of Education. (2006a). *Early learning for every child today: A framework for Ontario early childhood settings.* Toronto, Ontario: Queen's Printer for Ontario.

Ontario Ministry of Education. (2006b). *The Kindergarten program.* Toronto, Ontario: Queen's Printer for Ontario.

Ontario Ministry of Education. (2009). *Realizing the promise of diversity: Ontario's equity and inclusive education strategy.* Toronto, Ontario: Queen's Printer for Ontario.

Ontario Ministry of Education. (2010). *The full-day early learning Kindergarten program* (Draft Version). Toronto, Ontario: Queen's Printer for Ontario.

Ontario Ministry of Education. (2012). *Full-day Kindergarten: Memo summary*. Toronto, Ontario: Government of Ontario. Retrieved from www. edu.gov.on.ca

Ontario Ministry of Education (2013a). *Full-day Kindergarten study evaluation*. Toronto, Ontario. Retrieved from http://www.edu.gov.on.ca/kindergarten/theresearchisin.html

Ontario Ministry of Education (2013b). *A meta-perspective on the evaluation of full-day Kindergarten during the first two years of implementation*. Toronto, Ontario: Queen's Printer for Ontario.

Ontario Ministry of Education (2013c). *Think, Feel, Act: Lessons from Research about Young Children*. Toronto, Ontario: Queen's Printer for Ontario.

Ontario Ministry of Education (2014) *How does learning happen? Ontario's Pedagogy for the Early Years*. Toronto, Ontario: Queen's Printer for Ontario.

Pascal, C. (2009a). *Every child, every opportunity: Curriculum and pedagogy for the early learning program*. Toronto, Ontario: Government of Ontario.

Pascal, C. (2009b). *With our best future in mind: Implementing early learning in Ontario*. Toronto, Ontario: Government of Ontario.

Pellegrini, A. (1976). *The future of play theory: A multidisciplinary inquiry into the contributions of Brian Sutton-Smith*. New York, NY: State University of New York.

Pelletier, J. (2012a). *Key findings from year 1 of Full-Day Early Learning Kindergarten in Peel*. Toronto, Ontario: Dr. Eric Jackman Institute of Child Study, Ontario Institute for Studies in Education.

Pelletier, J. (2012b). *Key findings from year 2 of Full-Day Early Learning Kindergarten in Peel*. Toronto, Ontario: Dr. Eric Jackman Institute of Child Study, Ontario Institute for Studies in Education.

Pelletier, J. (2014). *Key findings from year 3 of Full-Day Early Learning Kindergarten in Peel*. Toronto, Ontario: Ontario Institute for Studies in Education.

Perlmutter, J. C., & Burrell (1995). Learning through play as well as through work. *Young Children Young Children, 50* (5), 14-21.

Piaget, J. (1927). *The first year of life of the child*. British Journal of Psychology, *18*, 92-120.

Piaget, J. (1950). *The psychology of intelligence*. London: Routledge and Kegan Paul.

Piaget, J. (1952). *The child's conception of number*. London: Routledge and Kegan Paul.

Piaget, J. (1962). *Play, dreams, and imitation in childhood*. New York, NY: Norton.

Piaget, J. (1969). *The mechanisms of perception*. London: Rutledge and Kegan Paul.

Piaget, J. (1972). *Science of education and the psychology of the child*. New York, NY: Viking.

Plutchik, R. (2003) *Emotions and Life: Perspectives from Psychology, Biology, and Evolution*. Washington, DC: American Psychological Association.

Ramachandran, V.S. (2011). *The tell-tale brain: Unlocking the mystery of human nature*. London, UK: William Heinemann.

Rutledge, D. (2000). Neurons and nurture in the early years. *Education Canada, 39*(4), 16-19.

Schonert-Reichl, K. A., & Lawlor, M.S. (2010). *The effects of a mindfulness-based education program on pre-and early adolescents' well-being, social and emotional competence*. Mindfulness. 1(3), 137-151.

Schonert-Reichl, K.A., Oberle, E., Lawlor, M. S., Abbott, D., Thomson, K., Oberlander, T.F., & Diamond, A. (2015). *Enhancing cognitive and social-emotional development through a simple-to-administer mindfulness-based school program for elementary school children: A randomized controlled trial*. Developmental Psychology, 51(1), 52.

Segal, M. (2004). *Creativity and personality type tools for understanding and inspiring the many voices of creativity*. Concord, ON: Career / Life Skills Resource Inc.

Shanker, Stuart. (2013) *Calm, Alert, and Learning – Classroom Strategies for Self-Regulation*. Toronto: Pearson Canada Inc.

Shanker, Stuart. (2017). *Self_Regulation: How to Help Your Child (And You) Break the Stress Cycle and Successfully Engage with Life.* Toronto: Penguin Random House

Steiner, R. (1965). *Education of the Child.* London: Rudolf Steiner Press.

Steiner, R. (1965). *Education of the Child.* London: Rudolf Steiner Press.

Steiner, R. (1994). *Theosophy: An introduction to the spiritual processes in human life and in the cosmos.* New York, NY: Anthroposophic Press.

Sutton-Smith, B. (1966). Piaget on play: A critique. *Psychological Review, 73,* 104-110.

Sutton-Smith, B. (1976). *The future of play theory: A multidisciplinary inquiry into the contributions of Brian Sutton-Smith.* New York, NY: State University of New York.

Sutton-Smith, B. (1997). *The ambiguity of play.* Cambridge, MA: First Harvard University Press.

Sylva K., Melhusih, E. Sammons, P., Siraj-Blatchford, I., & Taggart, B. (2004).*The effective provision of pre-school education (EPPE) Project.* London: OFES/Institute of Education. University of London.

The Laboratory School at the Dr. Eric Jackman Institute for Child Study. (2011). *Natural curiosity: Building children's understanding of the world through environmental inquiry*. Kingston, ON: Miracle Press Ltd.

Thompson, R. A. (2006b). The development of the person: Social understanding, relationships, self, conscience. In W. Damon & R. M. Lerner (Eds.), *Handbook of child psychology* (6th Ed., pp. 24-98), Vol. 3. Social, emotional, and personality development (N. Eisenberg, Vol. Ed.). New York, NY: Wiley.

Thompson, R. A. (2006c). Nurturing developing brains, minds, and hearts. In R. Lally& P. Mangione (Eds.), *Concepts of care: 20 essays on infant/toddler development and learning* (pp. 47-52). Sausalito, CA: WestEd.

Thompson, R. A., Goodvin, R., & Meyer, S. (2006). Social development: Psychological understanding, self-understanding, and relationships. In J. Luby (Ed.), *Handbook of preschool mental health: Development, disorders and treatment* (pp. 3-22). New York, NY: Guilford.

Thompson, R. A., & Lagatutta, K. (2006). Feeling and understanding: Early emotional development. In K. McCartney & D. Phillips (Eds.), *The Blackwell handbook of early childhood development* (pp. 317-337). Oxford, UK: Blackwell.

United Nations Educational, Scientific and Cultural Organization (UNESCO). (2008). *Inclusive education: The way of the future*. UNESCO International Conference on Education. November 25-28. Geneva: UNESCO.

UNICEF. (2010). *Fact Sheet: A summary of the rights under the convention on the rights of the child*. Article 31. Retrieved from http://www.unicef.org/crc.files/Rights_overview.pdf, accessed March 4, 2013.

United Nations—General Assembly. (1989). Session 44 Resolution 25. Convention on the Rights of the Child. 20 November 1989.

Van den Berg, A.R. (1986). Play theory. In Q. Fein& M. Rivkin (Eds.), *The young child at play*. Washington, DC: NAEYC.

Vanderlee, M.L, Youmans, S., Peters, R., & Eastabrook, J. (2012). Queen's Study. *Final report: Evaluation of the implementation of the Ontario full-day early learning kindergarten program*. Kingston: Queen's University. Retrieved from http://www.edu.gov.on.ca/kindergarten/FDELK_ReportFall2012.pdf

Vershueren, K., Doumen, S. & Buyse, E. (2012). Relationship with mother, teacher and peers: Unique and joint effects on young children's self-concept. *Attachment & Human Development* 14 (3), 233-248.

Vitale, J., & Len, Ihaleakala Hew. *Zero Limits–The Secret Hawaiian System for Wealth, Health, Peace & More*. (2007). Hoboken, NJ: John Wiley & Sons, Inc.

Vygotsky, L.S. (1934, 1986). *Thought and language*. A. Kozulin (Ed.). Cambridge, MA: MIT Press.

Vygotsky, L.S. (1978). *Mind in society: The development of higher psychological processes.* M.Cole, V. John-Steiner, S. Scribner, & E. Souberman (Eds.). Cambridge, MA: Harvard University Press.

Vygotsky, L. S. (1987). Thinking and speech. In R. W. Reiber & A. S. Carton (Eds.), (Trans., N. Minick), *The collected works of L. S. Vygotsky.* Vol. 1: Problems of general psychology. New York, NY: Plenum Press.

Vygotsky, L.S. (1998). *The collected works of L.S. Vygotsky.* R.W. Reiber (Ed.). Vol. 5: Child psychology. New York, NY: Plenum Press.

Wane, N. (2010). *Spirituality and schooling: Sociological and pedagogical implications in education.* Toronto, Ontario: Canadian Scholars' Press. Washington, V. (2002). Why early childhood matters now more than ever. *Early Childhood Today, 17*(3), 5.

Zull, J.E. (2002). *The art of changing the brain: Enriching the practice of teaching by exploring the biology of learning.* Stylus Publishing: Sterling, VA.

ACKNOWLEDGEMENTS

My journey as a learner, a researcher and an educator has bridged me to more than I could imagine. Becoming a mother was a major turning point driving an interest in child development. Seeing the world through a mother's lens opened my heart to children. Having my son and daughter to connect with at different ages and stages in life brought great joy and enhanced my world with each of their unique qualities. Thank you to both of you for your authentic presence and insightful interactions.

I am most appreciative of the inspirations from my family. My mother and father with their loving embrace, instilled values of kindness and compassion along with their shared wisdom to be ambitious and work hard to achieve my goals. My son and daughter who made me grow, think divergently and become a better human being. My husband, who with his humour, provided the much needed breaks when needed. My in-laws inspired me with their dedication to service and helping others. To my sister for always being my listening ear, confidant and guiding light. My brother, who is an amazing dad, showed me novel ideas and ways of being and my sister-in-law who shared creative styles as she captured moments so eloquently. To all of my nieces and nephews that brought many experiences to the forefront reminding me of all the precious family stories and shared memories that I hold as a collection of treasures in my life. My relatives in Canada and abroad provided much inspiration. Thank you to my grandparents and the power of heritage, ancestry, roots that help define who I am. To Mama and Mimi - divine souls - honoured and remembered. I am most grateful to all of you.

The love for learning instilled in me from childhood guided my work and allowed me to venture into the journey of an elementary school teacher. The joy of discovery with the exploration of music, painting, art activities, writing, designing, drawing, drama, dance along with presenting have allowed me to express myself in creative ways in the classroom. Sometimes it was not the experiences that followed conventions that made a difference but rather the different ones, those unique, the more unconventional that left an impression. Working with a diverse student community continued to challenge my thinking and I am grateful for that. Thank you to all my students who inspired me by sharing their life stories and opening up with such magnificence.

My educational research endeavours explored local, national and international innovations in education broadened my understanding and widened my lens. I am grateful to teaching and research colleagues who over the past decade have taught me new perspectives and practices. The meetings with policy makers were riveting and dynamic. The challenges, the joys and laughter over classroom commodore, advocacy on the picket lines for better education, the push for political changes to increase investments into the future of our children leave a deep impression. We rallied, advocated and made change a reality.

To the child – a mind filled with amazing and incredible

moments of wonderment. Creative thinking development always fascinated me; this book gave me the platform to share insight and knowledge while exploring the ingenuity of creativity. Of all the interactions the most fulfilling were the dialogues with children who made me smile and feel what they were feeling at that very moment. I thought more about the child's mind, their ever-changing and splendid perspectives - an authentic and pure view like no other. You are the light that radiates and shines in my heart.

The significance and influence of the community had a great impact on me. I am filled with much gratitude for those who supported me throughout my journey. Knowledge and wisdom not only allowed me to learn but also to share. Strong pillars of family, friends, time with researchers, book club contemplators, and teachers provided much inspiration for me to divulge into books, optimize classroom experiences, extend to community outreach projects while engaging deeply in research and academia.

The work with the Atkinson Centre at OISE provided great research experiences and opportunities. I am proud to be working as staff with such an amazing team of faculty, educators and researchers. Thank you to Kerry McCuaig who involved me in the significant and meaningful work that meant the world to me. I am grateful for you believing in me.

It was the simple observation of a butterfly that sometimes became the highlight of my day. Butterflies always had a magical presence for me. Bringing messages to me. By listening to the sound of the birds, observing them, watching them gracefully fly made me smile and directed my attention that glided me through this journey. Like a caterpillar that retreats in the chrysalis and undergoes a transformation I felt the release of my wings when writing. In the final stages the project took on a new dimension. By letting some things fade away I made room for other new things to take shape. Living my authentic truth and gaining a sense of alignment I could breathe and just be.

ABOUT THE AUTHOR

Dr. Ella Karia is currently working as an *Associate Researcher* with the Atkinson Centre for Society and Child Development at the Ontario Institute for Studies in Education, University of Toronto. Dr. Karia as an *Post-Doctoral Fellow* with the organization was involved in two major Canadian government funded educational projects: 1) The Early Learning and Child Care (ELCC) Innovation project examining Canada-wide innovations in education; 2) The 2020 Early Childhood Education Report (ECER) examining provincial comparisons of progress with investment in early years education. As a presenter at the Summer Institute on Early Childhood Development for the past three years she has been examining equity, access and quality in education. Engaging with educational researchers, policy-makers and educators in 2011, she worked as the Early Years Coordinator at the Department of Applied Psychology and Human Development focusing on literacy development practices and the value of professional development through the use of technology. In 2012, she worked on the project Women and Leadership in Higher Education at the Department of Humanities, Social Sciences and Social Justice Education. She received her Doctorate in Education from the University of Toronto in 2014. Dr. Karia's interest in advocacy for equity, parental engagement and social justice education is an integral part of her community involvement and research interests.

As a Certified Elementary School Teacher, for over a decade, with the Ontario College of Teachers, she continues to stay active teaching in the elementary classroom in the public school arena. Dr. Karia explores ways to improve pedagogy and instructional approaches by launching and leveraging creative and critical thinking skill development within her classroom. Working in primary and junior grades she leveraged her advocacy for student voice, creative approaches and the deepening of student curiosities with scientific inquiry. In 2015, she was selected to join a curriculum writing team at her school board. She was part of a team that published an Educator's Guide to Transformative Early Year Programming distributed to administrators and educators. Examining and reflecting closely on the needs and brain development of young children she conducted studies on educator's perspectives and gaining a deeper understanding of classroom practice and innovative teaching practices. She authored the book *Fostering Creativity* which is based on her own steadfast pursuit of learning through inquiry and play in the early years and its implications for child development highlights the critical skills for modern learners. *Exploring Creativity* shares insight on child development and youth empowerment beyond the early years.

At the university, over four years she worked with graduate students through the OISE mentorship program. Volunteering her time as an Executive Board Member, in the role of Vice President of a charitable children's choir and as a Co-Chair of a global educational charity she helped underprivileged children as a community advocate for global educational projects and raised funds to increase accessibility to schools. As an Independent Consultant for the Child

Development Resource Connection, Dr. Karia facilitates workshops for educators and presents at conferences. She is also an Editorial Member of the International Journal of Children's Spirituality and a Writer for the Conversation and a Senior Writer for a NGO aligning Sustainable Development Goals (SDG) that establishes a stronger value-based education. With a steadfast pursuit of multidimensional involvement in education Dr. Karia shares insight on how learning happens.

As an Educational Consultant she has consulted with families supporting educational endeavours and counselled many individuals as they find their pathways to discover their most empowered self. For educational consulting email Dr. Ella Karia at exploringcreativitywithkids@gmail.com.

CPSIA information can be obtained
at www.ICGtesting.com
Printed in the USA
BVHW091102290822
645316BV00002B/6